This book is dedicated to my family and especially my parents, Robert and Gerry Bell, who have continually given me support and encouragement for my work.

# Alberta's Metis Settlements Legislation

## An Overview of Ownership and Management of Settlement Lands

*Catherine E. Bell*

Canadian Plains Research Center
University of Regina
1994

Canadian Plains Research Center
University of Regina
Regina, Saskatchewan S4S 0A2
Canada

**Canadian Cataloguing in Publication Data**

Bell, Catherine Edith, 1961-

Alberta's Metis settlements legislation

(Canadian plains studies ; 27)

Includes bibliographical references.
ISBN 0-88977-081-6

1. Alberta. Metis Settlements Act. 2. Metis – Alberta – Legal status, laws, etc. 3. Metis – Alberta – Land tenure. I. University of Regina. Canadian Plains Research Center. II. Title. III. Series.

FC126.A3B44 1994   346.712304'32'08997   C94-920102-2
E92.B43  1994

Cover Design: Brian Mlazgar / Agnes Bray

Printed and bound in Canada by
Hignell Printing Limited, Winnipeg, Manitoba

Printed on acid-free paper

# ALBERTA'S METIS
# SETTLEMENTS LEGISLATION

# Contents

# Acknowledgements

The author gratefully acknowledges the valuable comments of David Elliott, Cameron Henry, Fred Martin, Dennis Surrendi and David Schneiderman. Thank you also to Kim Cordeiro, Lorie Huising and Louisa Maciuk for their patience and skill in typing the various drafts. A special thank you to the Metis Settlements Transition Authority and General Council for encouraging and supporting my work. It is our hope that this book will assist the general public, the private sector, government and aboriginal groups to understand the settlements legislation.

# 1 Introduction

On 1 November 1990, the government of Alberta enacted the *Metis Settlements Land Protection Act, Metis Settlements Act (MSA), Metis Settlements Accord Implementation Act,* and the *Constitution of Alberta Amendment Act, 1990.*[1] This legislation provides for protection of a collective land base for settlement members through an amendment to the constitution of Alberta, creation of a unique landholding system, development of local Metis government, a temporary mechanism for implementation of Metis control over local government and financial administration, and a financial commitment of $310 million to be allocated over a period of seventeen years. In addition, the province will provide grants matching specified revenues collected by the settlements and the settlements will have access to certain grants on the same basis as other local governments in Alberta. The legislative package is accompanied by a Co-Management Agreement which provides a framework for management of subsurface resources.[2]

The legislation is the result of a long history of negotiations between Metis leaders and the provincial government which draws on the existing settlement scheme and the desire of settlement Metis to own and govern settlement lands. As part of the final agreement, the Federation of Metis Settlements (Federation) agreed to stay a twenty-one-year-old lawsuit against Alberta which alleged that the province withheld and mismanaged funds arising from the sale of subsurface resources and that such funds were to be deposited in the Metis Settlements Trust Fund to be administered by the province for the benefit of the Metis.[3] The stay of proceedings is subject to the condition that "the Legislature does not enact any Act that repeals or amends the *Constitution of Alberta Amendment Act, 1990.*"[4]

The enactment of the settlements legislation is a significant event in Metis history for several reasons. The legislation represents a first in providing for collective ownership, legislated protection and constitutional protection of a land base for Metis people.[5] It also represents an unprecedented step towards Metis economic independence and local government. In some areas in Saskatchewan Metis people have effectively utilized their majority representation and have elected Metis mayors. Some attempts have also been made in Manitoba and Saskatchewan to accommodate the special concerns of northern Metis communities through devolution of authority to nonethnic regional or local government. However, this approach fails to guarantee Metis representation and leaves predominantly Metis communities open to the threat of non-Metis peoples settling in, and acquiring control over, traditional Metis lands.[6] Alberta's settlement Metis are the first Metis peoples to be guaranteed representative ethnic local and regional government over individual settlements and the entire settlement area. They are also the first to be delegated law-making and quasi-judicial powers defined by provincial legislation and exercisable within a defined Metis territory.

Alberta's initiatives also raise important constitutional issues. The settlements legislation is the first provincial legislative scheme to enact a comprehensive rights regime for aboriginal peoples. Alberta claims it has jurisdiction to enact this legislation under sections 92(8) and 92(13) of the *Constitution Act, 1867* which provide for provincial jurisdiction in respect to local government and property and civil rights.[7] However, s.91(24) of the *Constitution Act, 1867* gives federal Parliament jurisdiction over "Indians, and lands reserved for the Indians." The term "Indians" is not defined, but it is clear that the term includes a larger group of aboriginal peoples than those included in the federal *Indian Act* regime.[8] If the Metis are s.91(24) Indians, Alberta's Metis legislation could exceed the constitutional powers of the provincial legislature by singling out an aboriginal people for special treatment, a role which is arguably within the exclusive domain of the federal government pursuant to s.91(24). The Alberta settlement Metis have indicated their willingness and preference to negotiate with the province of Alberta rather than the federal government. The current federal government's acceptance of the constitutional validity of the Alberta scheme opens the door for similar arrangements across Canada, but at the same time it could foster provincial unrest. Some provinces have argued that Metis are a federal responsibility under s.91(24).[9] The issue of responsibility is crucial to provinces with significant Metis populations or a limited source of public lands and revenues for the settlement of claims.

Another constitutional issue raised by the settlements legislation is whether it settles claims arising from Metis aboriginal rights and thereby constitutes a modern treaty or land claims agreement protected by s.35(3) of the *Constitution Act, 1982*.[10] The issue of Metis aboriginal rights is extremely complex and has received limited judicial attention and academic consideration. The absence of aboriginal rights language in the legislation, the process adopted for constitutional entrenchment of the Metis land base, and the preamble to the *Constitution of Alberta Amendment Act, 1990* suggest that Metis aboriginal rights are not to be affected and the legislation is not a modern land claims agreement. However, the

2

legislation is the result of an agreement between the province and the Federation preceded by several years of negotiation in which the Metis aboriginal rights were discussed. Further, the substance of the legislation deals with some rights traditionally attributed to aboriginal peoples.

According to Fred Martin, counsel for the Federation, aboriginal rights language was avoided in the end to prevent other governments or aboriginal groups from challenging the provincial initiative.[11] Aware of the potential constitutional difficulties arising from the characterization and implementation of provincial legislation, the Federation eventually settled on a pragmatic results-oriented approach to obtain the desired results: a land base and greater economic and political autonomy. Rather than insist upon the recognition of aboriginal rights, the approach focussed on results. Fred Martin, counsel for the settlements describes the results-oriented approach and Metis strategy as follows:

> A person seeking government action can develop a strategy focused either on rights or results. The 'results' orientation means that the paramount concern is to achieve a specific result without much attention paid to the government's motivations. The source of the government's mandate is not critical; the only real concern is that it accept some responsibility. The 'rights' orientation is quite different, with paramount attention concentrated on the source of the government's mandate, since the mandate of the constitution conveys the legal right. ...

> The history of the Metis settlements is one of pragmatic, results oriented leadership. Rights have been asserted and assiduously protected, but the driving concern has been results. Metis leaders have not insisted that the government recognize a right and act in response to that right. Rather the emphasis has been on action, leaving the government to sort out for itself whether its mandate was conscience or constitution.[12]

This book reviews the systems of ownership and management of Metis settlement lands created as a result of this approach within a broad historical, political and legal context. As land ownership and management arrangements cannot be properly understood in isolation, the book begins with an overview of the historical process through which Alberta's settlement Metis acquired title to a secure land base and local government over their territories. This is followed by an overview of the Metis lands registry system, Metis ownership and landholding systems, land use planning and resource management. The book concludes with a discussion of broader legal issues arising from the application of constitutional law and the common law of aboriginal rights.

# Legislative History of the Metis Settlements

# 2

## THE PEOPLE OF THE METIS SETTLEMENTS

As a result of federal policy adopted in the late 1800s, Metis in what are now Saskatchewan, Manitoba and Alberta were offered treaty if they lived among and were accepted by Indian communities. Others were offered scrip, a certificate issued to individual Metis redeemable for land or money.[13] Scrip distribution proved to be an inadequate procedure for settling Metis grievances and providing for the welfare of Metis communities. As a result, many Metis were left impoverished and Metis communities throughout the Prairies lost their lands. The issue of whether the scrip distribution system was constitutionally valid and justly compensated the Metis for the loss of their lands is the subject of substantial academic commentary and is currently the subject of litigation.[14]

Following the North-West Metis Resistance of 1885, Father Lacombe approached the federal government for funding to establish a farming colony to assist destitute Metis peoples. In 1895, the colony of St. Paul des Metis was established by the government of Canada in northern Alberta, but after ten years of operation and without consulting the Metis, the managing board declared the colony a failure and it was opened for public homesteading. Some have suggested that the real reason for the failure was the loss of faith in the project by Father Therien, the manager of the colony, and his desire to establish a French Canadian colony.[15] The colony was opened for homesteading during the same year that the province of Alberta was created. However, the federal government continued to issue scrip to Metis in Alberta until 1921.[16]

Some of the Metis dispossessed by the opening of St. Paul des Metis settled on unoccupied Crown lands in the Fishing Lake area.[17] Other northern communities were established, composed of descendants of the Metis Nation for whom the scrip system had failed to provide a land base or adequate means of support, and converted status Indians who surrendered their entitlements under federal Indian legislation in exchange for scrip.[18] In the 1930s, these communities suffered as a result of the Depression, illness and the threat of losing their land and way of life to settlers migrating to the northern areas of Alberta from the plains. During this period, Joseph Dion petitioned the provincial government on behalf of the Metis for assistance in "obtaining land, education, medical care and free hunting and fishing permits"[19] and shortly thereafter the Metis Association of Alberta was formed. The efforts of Metis political leaders resulted in the appointment of a provincial commission with a mandate to investigate the health, education, relief and general welfare of the Metis population of the province. Although invited to participate in the inquiry, the federal government refused on the basis that "half-breeds" are not a federal responsibility.[20]

## THE EWING COMMISSION

The Ewing Commission held hearings throughout Alberta for approximately one year and submitted its report in February 1936. The tone and recommendations of the Ewing Commission were paternalistic. The Commission concluded that if the Metis had special rights arising from aboriginal ancestry, such rights were extinguished through the distribution of scrip.[21] It was clear that the Commission was not responding to Metis title claims to land; rather, it was responding to the needs of a destitute Metis and non-status Indian population.[22] Consequently, the Commission recommended allotment of Crown land for use and occupation by the "half-breed" population as farm colonies and developed proposals for the supervision of settlement activities. Recognizing that the Metis were the original inhabitants of the proposed settlement areas, the Commission implicitly acknowledged the existence of group rights and recommended that the Metis be given preference over nonresidents in the harvesting of fur, game and fish.[23]

According to Douglas Sanders, the following assumptions influenced the findings of the Commission:

1. Metis claims to Indian title were extinguished by the scrip distribution system;

2. Metis and non-status Indians were the responsibility of the province;

3. The Metis of northern Alberta were asserting needs not rights; and

4. The response to those needs would involve land allocation.[24]

In short, the Commission focussed on perceived social needs rather than legal rights.

## THE *METIS BETTERMENT ACT*

In November 1938, following the recommendations of the Ewing Commission, the province of Alberta enacted the *Metis Population Betterment Act*,[25] later changed to the *Metis Betterment Act*. The definition of a Metis person under the Act was a "person of mixed white and Indian blood but [not] ... an Indian or a non-treaty Indian as defined in the

*Indian Act.*"[26] A joint Metis/government committee selected lands to be set aside as settlement areas. Of the initial settlement areas set aside, eight remain, with a combined total area of 1.25 million acres.[27] A minister of the Crown was given the responsibility for the economic and social development of the settlements, but the scheme envisioned was for the Minister and the settlements to work cooperatively in the formulation of programs for the betterment of the Metis. Regulations concerning hunting and trapping rights on settlement lands could be enacted by the Lieutenant Governor in Council. The Act also provided a framework for the creation of settlement associations and the assumption of limited powers of government. Settlement associations were authorized to establish settlement constitutions outlining conditions for "membership, elections, board meetings and other details of managing the settlement associations."[28] They also had by-law making powers limited by the scope of individual settlement constitutions and requiring approval by the Minister.

Significant amendments were made to the Act in 1940. Detailed administration was defined through government regulation rather than informal cooperative schemes. This resulted in increased control by the government and increased Metis dependency on bureaucratic processes. The government retained significant regulatory powers including the right to set conditions for occupation, use and development of settlement lands, and disposition of timber. The Minister also had a broad power to pass any regulation that concerned the betterment of Metis settlers, lands or associations.[29] Other changes included:

1. The Minister was granted authority to designate settlement areas as Improvement Districts enabling the Lieutenant Governor in Council to assess taxes and terminate rights of occupation for unpaid taxes;

2. Taking security against property of settlement members was prohibited and Metis personal property was exempted from seizure unless the property at issue was purchased under a conditional sales contract;

3. "Metis" was defined as a person with a minimum of one quarter Indian blood and the condition that only destitute Metis could join a settlement association was repealed; and

4. The interest of a settlement member in settlement land could descend to his or her spouse or children who are Metis and become settlement members.[30]

The next significant amendments to the Act occurred in 1952. The powers of individual settlement associations to provide for the election of five settlement board members to serve on boards of settlement associations and the Act's reference to the board's authority to control "the business and affairs of the association" were removed.[31] Instead, the Minister was authorized to appoint two board members and the local provincially appointed supervisor was deemed the chair.[32] Only two members of the settlement board were to be elected by members of the settlement association.

In the 1960s, four Metis settlements were removed from the settlement regime (Touchwood, Marlboro, Cold Lake and Wolf Lake). Of these areas only Wolf Lake was occupied and occupants of that settlement were relocated to other settlement areas.[33] In 1979, a further amendment converted the Metis Population Betterment Trust Account to the Metis Settlements Trust Fund.[34] With the exception of these changes, the *Metis Betterment Act* remained essentially unchanged until the proclamation of the new legislative package in 1990.

Government officials and the Metis simply ignored those sections of the Act that were unworkable. However, the more the system was ignored, the more the uncertainty of Metis authority and friction between government officials and the settlement Metis increased.[35] As a result, in 1972 a provincial task force was struck to examine the legislation. Practical assumption of administrative responsibilities, recommendations of the Task Force (discussed below), and further feelings of distrust arising from the seizure of Metis files in the natural resources litigation[36] fuelled greater political organization and lobbying by settlement Metis for a new deal.

## THE 1970s AND PROPOSALS FOR REFORM

In 1969 the provincial Metis Task Force began its review of the Metis legislation. In 1972 the Task Force completed its report.[37] The Task Force recommended that the Metis settlements move toward a form of local self-government in the form of Improvement Districts, that the setting aside of lands for the Metis be a perpetual commitment, and that "future development of the Metis Settlements, must clearly be identified with the development of the people, rather than economic projects or programs."[38] The Task Force also stipulated four principles to be considered in future dealings with the Metis:

1. Community development belongs to the people;
2. The community needs ready access to resources;
3. Pilot undertakings should be employed to initiate the movement toward local self-government; and
4. Community development must begin with the culture and value system of the people and move forward from there.[39]

Following the Task Force report the Metis Development Branch in the Department of Health and Social Services adopted a policy to reduce its administrative role and to devolve more responsibility to the settlements.

By 1979, most settlement councils had assumed significant administrative powers and responsibility for the delivery of local housing, education, economic, and cultural programs. Following an investigation into the seizure of settlement files by representatives of the Metis Settlements Branch in 1979, the provincial Ombudsman recommended that a joint Metis/government commission be formed to review the administration of the *Metis Betterment Act* and that administration of the Act be transferred to the Department of Municipal Affairs. This was done in 1980, and in 1982 a joint committee chaired by the Honourable Dr. Grant MacEwan was established, composed of an equal number of Metis and government appointers.[40] The purpose of the joint committee was to "act in an advisory capacity and in particular to review the *Metis Betterment Act* and Regulations and make recommendations which would allow for political, cultural, social and economic development on Metis Settlements."[41]

## THE MACEWAN COMMITTEE

### The Legal and Political Climate

Unlike the report of the Task Force, the MacEwan Report was compiled in a national political climate which recognized Metis as aboriginal peoples. During this period, aboriginal rights were recognized and affirmed in the Canadian constitution and Metis were identified as an aboriginal people of Canada. Further, the new Canadian constitution required the First Ministers to hold a series of conferences to define the scope and content of aboriginal rights.[42] In response to these developments, in 1982 the Federation published a position paper entitled *Metisism: A Canadian Identity*.[43] *Metisism* asserts Metis aboriginal rights to land and government. In this document the key components of Metis aboriginal title were identified as "land and resources, distinct political status, social development, cultural development, and economic development."[44] An interesting legal argument was also developed to support the position that Metis title in settlement lands is similar to Indian title in reserve lands, vesting title in the Crown and beneficial use in the Metis.[45] Although the paper accepted provincial jurisdiction in determining the political status of the settlements, the paper evidences a desire for the federal government to be involved in the protection of Metis aboriginal rights.

The Metis also had several concerns arising from the administration of the *Metis Betterment Act*. According to the Metis, the government had too much control over the administration and development of settlement lands. Despite the existing policy of devolving administrative responsibilities to the settlements, the Metis remained subject to the political will of the government. Since the settlement boards were initially established as advisory bodies and their role changed through informal policy rather than legislative amendment, their legal status was uncertain. This became of increasing importance as it cast doubt on the ability of the board to enter legally binding contracts and the ability of the board to sue or be sued. The issue became significant in the natural resources trust fund litigation where the Crown successfully blocked the initial law suit. The Crown argued that the action should be brought against the Minister of Public Welfare, that consent to commence proceedings against the Minister must be given by the Lieutenant Governor in Council and that the right to bring an action, if any right exists, lies with the Metis Settlement Associations and not with the individual members thereof. The Alberta Supreme Court agreed that the Minister of Public Welfare was the proper defendant and that the required consent of the Lieutenant Governor in Council had not been obtained. On the issue of the capacity to sue, Mr. Justice Riley held that the Settlement Associations were creatures of statute and that a proposal or by-law respecting the feasibility of bringing an action to sue the Crown would have to be approved by the Minister. In his opinion it was "abundantly plain that the final control of the Metis association was designed to rest with the department of public welfare and final discretion in all important matters lies with the minister of public welfare."[46] The associations, or any member thereof only had capacity to sue if permission was obtained from the Minister.

The settlement Metis also had no control over economic development and administration of resource trust funds. In their opinion, the trust funds were not being administered for the benefit of the settlement Metis; the province was more concerned with the exploitation of settlement resources than the well-being of settlement communities.[47] In the litigation the settlement Metis alleged that the provincial government had a legal obligation to administer the funds as trustees for the benefit of Metis peoples arising from the language of the legislation and their status as aboriginal peoples. The position of the Crown was that the creation of a trust was contrary to the intent of the legislation, the Metis did not have a legal interest capable of forming the subject matter of a trust, and the obligations of the Crown are political, not legal. In the alternative, the Crown asserted that the Metis did not have aboriginal rights and that the actions of the Crown did not give rise to breach of trust or fiduciary obligation.[48]

In order to free themselves from economic and political dependency, the Metis sought control, through litigation and negotiation, of settlement resource revenues, powers of government analogous to those exercised by municipalities, and protection for traditional economic pursuits such as hunting, fishing, trapping and gathering. In published position papers and the natural resources litigation, the Federation asserted the right as an aboriginal people to determine their own membership. It was believed that self-determination was integral to their continued existence as a people.[49] Of particular concern was the inability of the settlement communities to prevent the withdrawal of settlement lands from the community and the alteration of settlement boundaries. It was believed that Metis government and survival of the Metis as a distinct aboriginal people were dependent upon the existence of a secure land base where the Metis community could grow and continue through successive generations. For these reasons, throughout the negotiation process the Federation pushed for title to be issued in a Metis collective entity to ensure that the Metis would always maintain collective ownership of settlement lands.

The Metis also asserted that they were owners of the land and resources in the settlement areas.[50] At the very least, they asserted, the land was held by the province for the benefit of the Metis and the Metis had usufructuary title to settlement lands similar to that enjoyed by Indian bands under the federal *Indian Act*.[51] The combined effect of the creation of a usufruct and the subsequent recognition of Metis as an aboriginal people in s.35(2) of the *Constitution Act, 1982* was to create an aboriginal right to land protected by s.35(1) of the constitution.[52] It became clear during the course of the natural resources trust fund litigation that the province disagreed. In their opinion, Metis title was dependent on creation and recognition by the province. While not denying that the Metis are an aboriginal people, the province maintained that any aboriginal rights they may have had were extinguished prior to the constitutional protection of aboriginal rights in 1982. Further, they maintained that the *Metis Betterment* legislation did not create or recognize aboriginal interests in settlement lands.[53]

The litigation also revealed that the Metis and the province had differing opinions on the legal nature of the *Metis Betterment Act*. In the opinion of the Metis, the legislation grew in response to political agitation for the recognition of Metis rights and the failure of the federal government to protect Metis interests. To the Metis, the establishment of the settlements represented "recognition by the Government of Alberta of historic Metis political and aboriginal rights."[54] The Act was viewed as an agreement between the Metis and the province that was subsequently altered and administered in a manner contrary to the agreement and the spirit of cooperation envisioned by the Act.[55] In support of this position the Metis emphasized accounts of elders and the preamble of the Act which provides that the legislation evolved: "by means of conferences and negotiations between the Government of the province and representatives of the metis population of the province."[56] On the other hand, the province maintained that the Act was not an agreement but welfare legislation enacted by the province for the benefit of disadvantaged citizens. Any rights that the Metis may have had were considered extinguished prior to its enactment.[57]

## Recommendations of the MacEwan Committee

The report of the MacEwan Committee was submitted to the Minister of Municipal Affairs in July 1984. The recommendations of the MacEwan Committee arose from consultations with members of the Metis settlements and addressed some of the specific concerns of the Metis in suggested provisions for a new *Metis Settlements Act*.[58] Recommendations were made without prejudice to matters before the courts.[59] The legislation proposed was intended to reflect the existing government policy of devolution of responsibility and to address specific concerns of the Metis arising out of the administration of the former legislation. Although the preamble to the legislation proposed by the MacEwan Committee recognized the aboriginal ancestry of the Metis and their distinct role in the history and culture of the province of Alberta, in substance it reflected a pragmatic approach to achieving results without being tangled in complex legal analysis and assertion of constitutional rights.[60] These issues were left to be resolved by the courts and the ongoing First Ministers' meetings established to define the scope of aboriginal and treaty rights entrenched in the new Canadian constitution.

The terms of reference for the Committee were stipulated by the Minister of Municipal Affairs in a letter dated 2 April 1982 to Dr. Grant MacEwan and all committee members. The work program of the committee was stated as follows:

1. A review of background material;

2. A detailed examination of the Metis Betterment Act and Regulations;

3. A review of the current political, health, educational, cultural, and economic situation of the Metis Settlements;

4. An examination of future alternatives for Metis Settlements;

5. The development of models in terms of local government, land holding, social organization and economic opportunity on Metis Settlements;

6. The establishment of guiding principles for the drafting of legislation which would allow for political, cultural, social and economic development on Metis Settlements;

7. A review of draft legislation; and

8. The preparation of a final report to the Minister.[61]

The committee recommended legislative changes with the following principles in mind:

1. the Metis represent a unique cultural group in Canada, an aboriginal people recognized in the Constitution, and a group that played a major role in the development of Western Canada;

2. because the culture and lifestyle of the Metis settlements is inextricably linked to the land, a Metis settlement land base is the cornerstone on which to build and maintain the social, cultural and economic strength of the Metis settlers;

3. given a unique culture and land base of the Metis Settlement Areas, the Metis can best achieve the mutual goal of self-reliant integration, without homogenization, by a legislative framework enabling the maximum practicable local self-government of the land base;

4. it would not be practical to include in Metis settlement local government the full scope of powers required to deal with matters such as health, education, social services and economic development, but even in these cases the uniqueness of the culture and its problem solving traditions should be respected by Government bodies exercising the power.[62]

Some of the more significant proposals in the draft *Metis Settlements Act* recommended in the MacEwan Report can be summarized as follows:

1. Title to the surface of settlement lands in a settlement area is granted to the individual settlements but title to mines and minerals is left to be resolved by the natural resources trust fund litigation. Subject to this exception, natural resources are vested in the settlements. Settlement lands are brought within the Alberta land titles system. Restrictions are also placed on disposition and boundary alterations without consent of the Minister and 90 percent of the adult members of the settlements.

2. The rights of occupancy of settlement members are modelled on the old legislation which recognized rights of exclusive occupancy on a temporary basis while making improvements necessary to acquire a certificate of occupancy. A certificate of occupancy grants a right to exclusive occupancy so long as the holder is a settlement member. The certificate can be transmitted by will but cannot be leased to another member without approval of the council. It is anticipated that the conditions necessary to obtain certificates of occupancy will be established by the settlements.

3. Metis persons are defined as any person of aboriginal ancestry who identifies with Metis history and culture. Subject to a few exceptions, the recommended legislation provides that individual settlements are to control membership.

4. Settlements are governed by a settlement council consisting of five elected adult members. Election procedures are based in part on the *Local Authorities Election Act*.[63] However, the Lieutenant Governor in Council

may make election regulations. The Committee proposes a regulation which would create a staggered election system where two councillors are elected each year and the remainder for a term of two or three years.

5. Disqualification provisions and conflict of interest provisions are modelled on provincial municipal legislation. A council is also granted by-law making powers necessary "for the peace, order and good government of the settlement; for promoting health, safety, morality and welfare of residents of the settlement; and for the protection of life or property."[64] By-laws consistent with the legislation must be presented at a public meeting of the members for approval. Councils are also given jurisdiction to pass by-laws concerning hunting, fishing, trapping and gathering. Councils were also given the authority to grant leases, *profits à prendre* and other interests to nonmembers.

6. Disputes concerning land allocation and membership in settlements are to be resolved by a Senate of Elders established for each settlement. Again, a staggered election system is recommended.

7. The resource trust fund is to be managed by a corporate body (Trustees of the Metis Settlements Resource Trust Fund) composed of the chairmen of each Senate of Elders and an additional person to be appointed by the councils. The recommended legislation also envisions that a common resource development policy is to be established. Certain powers of the Trustees are stipulated and the Trustees are empowered to enlist the Minister's assistance to ensure proper financial administration. Guidelines for borrowing and spending by individual settlement councils are also specified.

8. The taking of security against settlement lands is prohibited but the former prohibition against taking security in and seizing personal property of the settlement members is removed. Assuming an investment is approved, the resource trust fund can be used as security.

9. Recognizing that local control of access and use of settlement lands is necessary to secure a land base and traditional resources, the legislation recommended that nonsettlement members, other than government officials, must obtain the permission of the settlement council to access settlement lands. In the event of conflict, the proposed legislation is given priority over provincial surface rights legislation.

In the opinion of the Committee, it was not practical for local government to have jurisdiction over health, education, and social services.[65] However, the committee recognized the desirability of educating all children in the area about Metis history and culture, the need for special training for social service and health workers to enhance greater knowledge and sensitivity toward Metis culture, and extending existing economic development programs in areas such as business and forestry development.[66] Problems not identified by the Committee, but clear upon the reading of the proposals include:

1. The land base of the Metis and local government remained vulnerable to the will of the legislature. The government could repeal the legislation and unilaterally destroy the scheme at any time unless arguments could be successfully made that the proposed legislation constituted a treaty or land claims agreement protected by s.35(1) of the *Constitution Act, 1982.*

2. The Committee failed to address the financing of self-government initiatives. Substantial revenues were in limbo because of the natural resource litigation. Restrictions were placed on borrowing and money derived from surface revenues was insufficient to support the transition.

3. Constitutional issues relating to provincial jurisdiction, constitutional status of Metis settlement lands and the legal nature of the previous legislation were not specifically addressed. If anything, the issues were enhanced through the new assumptions that were introduced in the formulation of the proposals. The preamble to the proposed legislation recognized that the Metis are an aboriginal people and that lands set aside for them were intended to provide a secure foundation for future generations.[67] The legislation also contained culturally based components such as a dispute resolution panel composed of elders and control by settlements over hunting, fishing, trapping and gathering. The inclusion of aboriginal rights language coupled with the recognition of property, cultural and political rights in the proposed legislation and subsequent drafts raised the issue of whether the new legislative regime could constitute a treaty or modern land claims agreement.

## RESOLUTION 18

Despite previous differences between the Federation and the province, the provincial government responded positively to the MacEwan Report. The report gave rise to a fresh set of negotiations between the province and the Metis with a view toward implementing the Committee's recommendations. Although the settlements recognized the jurisdictional problems associated with bilateral provincial/Metis negotiations, they maintained a preference for working with the province which they believed was more responsive to the needs and aspirations of Metis settlers than a distant federal government. As it became clear that the constitutional conferences were not going to assist in the clarification of Metis rights, the province and the Metis began to focus on a "made in Alberta" approach which would achieve Metis aspirations for self-government and provide constitutional protection for the existing land base. In talks between the Federation and the province, the question of provincial legislative jurisdiction was "generally ignored on the basis that it is a question for the courts and not something either party [could] do anything about."[68]

Throughout the First Ministers' Conferences on Aboriginal Matters, Premier Lougheed maintained that Metis issues should be resolved through provincial initiatives. Even if the Metis fell within federal jurisdiction, he maintained this conclusion would not solve anything as the federal government's decision to assume responsibility under s.91(24) is discretionary and would likely not be exercised.[69]

In 1985, the Federation and Premier Lougheed agreed to protect settlement lands through an amendment to the *Alberta Act*.[70] The agreement was conditional upon the settlements developing fair and democratic procedures for membership and land allocations. The framework for the "made in Alberta" approach was incorporated in a unanimous resolution of the Alberta Legislative Assembly on 3 June 1985 (Resolution 18).[71] The Resolution called for transfer of settlement lands to existing Metis settlement associations or such appropriate Metis corporate entities to be determined, without prejudice to the Metis settlement litigation. The contemplated transfer was subject to the reservation of mines and minerals to the province. The Resolution also envisioned a measure of self-government based upon membership criteria and the composition of governing bodies proposed by the Metis, the introduction of new legislation and an extraordinary amendment to the *Alberta Act* to ensure constitutional protection of the lands transferred.[72] The guiding principles for drafting the new legislation were:

> to respect the traditions of the settlements, to remedy problems created by current legislation, and as far as possible, to keep in the new Act the institutions and processes that had been found to work in the past.[73]

### RESPONSE OF THE FEDERATION TO RESOLUTION 18

Following these developments, the Federation embarked on a research and consultation process to develop the appropriate criteria for landholding systems and self-government. The initial response of the Metis to Resolution 18 is published in a discussion paper entitled *By Means of Conferences and Negotiations We Ensure Our Rights*.[74] The paper contains an historical discussion of the Metis concept of government and a proposal for a new *Metis Settlements Act* intended to constitute a "compromise between the government's need to maintain legislative authority and the settlements' need to have the capacity to protect their culture and their lands."[75] The proposed legislation established a framework for qualification and termination of membership, transfer of title, development of internal landholding systems, and establishment of four distinct branches of Metis government exercising legislative, administrative and quasi-judicial functions: individual settlement councils, an elders' committee, *ad hoc* Metis arbitration tribunals and an elected Okimawiwin (a general council composed of all members elected to the settlement councils). The first two bodies were intended to exercise jurisdiction within the territorial boundaries of individual settlement lands and the latter within the entire settlement area.

In the proposal, the supreme legislative authority is Okimawiwin. Details concerning elections, qualifications, terms of office, meetings and procedures are modelled after provincial municipal legislation (with slight variation).[76] The powers of the Okimawiwin are very extensive under this proposal. First, it is given power to enact policies by way of special resolution respecting land use, trapping, health, education, membership procedures and administration of the trust fund. Okimawiwin policy on hunting, gathering and trapping is given priority over provincial legislation. Individual settlement councils are granted by-law making authority similar to that recommended by the MacEwan Committee, with the proviso that by-laws conform with Okimawiwin policy. Second, fee simple title in the settlement areas is to be vested in Okimawiwin. Third, Okimawiwin is to administer the new Metis Settlements Resources Trust Fund. Finally, it is also responsible for establishing and maintaining a separate registry for interests in settlement lands.

The proposal also creates an elders' committee and *ad hoc* Metis arbitration tribunals for the purpose of resolving land and membership disputes. Conditions for the election, replacement and removal of elders are also outlined. The elders' committee is intended to provide a mediating role on issues of membership and land allocation. Decisions of the elders' committee can be appealed to *ad hoc* appeal tribunals appointed through the agreement of the parties to the dispute, Okimawiwin and, in some cases, the Minister. The composition, jurisdiction and remedial powers of the tribunals are also addressed.[77]

Proposals concerning title and disposition of settlement lands vary from the MacEwan recommendations. Rather than vest title in the individual settlements, collective ownership of all settlement lands is vested in Okimawiwin. Further, the proposal prohibits taking security in settlement lands and transferring lands except by cession to the province. Cession must be requested by a settlement council resolution and approved by a special resolution of Okimawiwin and 90 percent of the adult settlement members of the settlement concerned.[78] Certificate of Okimawiwin (aboriginal) title to the lands is to be issued in the name of Okimawiwin pursuant to the Alberta *Land Titles Act,*[79] but a special registry is proposed for the recording of Metis titles and other interests with respect to settlement lands. Details relating to the establishment of the registry, its operation and prioritization of interests are not addressed. Individual settlement members are entitled to apply for a memorandum of allocation which grants the holder the right of exclusive use and occupancy for a period of five years. Issuance of memoranda of allocation are conditional upon compliance with stipulations to be detailed in settlement by-laws and Okimawiwin land use policy. Where lands have been improved or cultivated in accordance with terms stipulated for the allocation, members can apply for a certificate of occupancy. The circumstances under which memoranda of allotment and certificates of occupancy can be cancelled are specified. Details regarding restrictions on transfer and inheritability of Metis interests are not specifically addressed.[80]

## ALBERTA-METIS SETTLEMENTS ACCORD: A NEW LEGISLATIVE FRAMEWORK

The bare-bones legislation proposed by the MacEwan Committee and the response of the Metis to Resolution 18 were the basis for further negotiations. Workshops were held on each settlement to discuss the proposals. Some were concerned that the proposals did not guarantee the rights of off-settlement Metis. Others were concerned that the Okimawiwin had too much power. A coalition of eastern settlement members, who were dissatisfied with the operations of their councils, formed to voice their dissatisfaction with the new scheme.[81] Another difficulty was the inability to address the question of financing. At this time the legislation and the lawsuit were being treated as exclusive parallel processes and the province was reluctant to address financing of the settlement government as long as the lawsuit was outstanding. Further, the Federation wanted to ensure that settlement members understood the proposals. As a result, the target date for the implementation of Resolution 18 at the end of 1987 was not met.

Throughout this process, negotiations continued between the Federation and the province. The negotiations resulted in the drafting of Bill 64, the *Metis Settlements Act*, and Bill 65, the *Metis Settlements Land Act* which were introduced into the Legislative Assembly on 5 July 1988.[82] Shortly before the introduction of the draft legislation, the government decided to link the trust fund lawsuit to the proposed legislation. The government indicated that it wanted the litigation settled in or out of court and that the commitments in Resolution 18 would not be fulfilled unless the lawsuit was settled.[83] Confident that a settlement to the litigation would be reached, Bills 64 and 65 were introduced.

The intention was to introduce enabling, rather than comprehensive, legislation.[84] The bills adopt several of the Metis proposals, but alter the amount of political autonomy proposed by the Metis. Further, details concerning membership, landholding systems, and dispute resolution are left to ministerial regulations enacted in cooperation with the Metis. Fred Martin describes the four cornerstones of the contemplated legislation as follows:

1. Constitutionally protected Metis lands set aside as settlement areas;

2. Settlement councils responsible for local government in the Settlement Areas, with additional powers to make decisions on membership and land allocation (subject to appeal);

3. A central land and trust fund holding body (the General Council) responsible for addressing common concerns of the settlement councils — such as the administration of the Trust Fund and the establishing of common policies with respect to land use planning, resource development, etc;

4. Provincial jurisdiction, consistent with the protection of the Constitution, over lands and institutions.[85]

Bill 64 provided a framework for local government. The Metis proposal for division of powers between a central policy-making body and individual settlements is retained. Settlement associations are established as corporations with the legal capacities of a natural person.[86] The Bill provides for the election of a five-person settlement council for each settlement and details their manner of operation and by-law making powers.[87] A significant variation from the provincial municipal model is the staggered election system and the requirement that by-laws be approved at a public meeting before they become effective.[88] The Bill also establishes a General Council with policy-making authority with respect to matters affecting the interests of all eight settlements. This component is rooted in Metis practice. Over the years, the Metis established the practice of gathering all council members from the various settlements to address issues of common interest to the settlement. Although it had no legal status, the policies it adopted were generally accepted by the settlement community.[89]

Under the Bill, unless provided otherwise, policies must be made, amended or repealed by a special resolution supported by 75 percent of the settlement corporations. Policies relating to hunting, gathering, trapping and fishing must be approved by an order of the Lieutenant Governor in Council. Other policies are subject to ministerial veto but the Minister also has regulatory power to determine which policies are not subject to veto. With the exception of hunting, trapping, fishing and gathering policies passed in consultation and approval of the Minister, General Council Policy must conform with provincial law and is inoperative to the extent of inconsistency.[90] The veto power has a trickling down effect to by-law making powers as individual settlement by-laws must conform with General Council Policy and are invalid to the extent of inconsistency.[91] Details for the establishment of an appeal tribunal are left to regulation.[92] The understanding is that the appeal tribunal, composed of Metis and government representatives, will exercise the powers that would have been exercised by the proposed Council of Elders and *ad hoc* arbitration tribunals in the resolution of local problems. The Minister is also empowered to make regulations concerning membership and financial matters.[93]

Some provisions concerning ownership and allocation of Metis lands are also contained in Bill 64. In particular, it addresses the withdrawal of Metis lands from the Alberta land titles system, limits on disposition of settlement lands, exemption from seizure and surface entry for the purposes of extracting subsurface resources. Details respecting land use, planning, allocation and the establishment of the Metis Settlement Land Registry are left to regulation.[94] Bill 65 addresses the transfer of title of the entire settlement area to General Council, and conditions on and reservations from title, disposition and expropriation.

The bills died on the order paper, but their content and the litigation continued to be the subject of negotiation and in January and February 1989 an agreement was finally reached. In June 1989, the provincial government announced that an Accord was proposed which would result in the lawsuit being dropped and that the Metis would be receiving $310 million over a period of seventeen years to support governance and operation of the settlement. Bills 64 and 65 also comprised part of the new deal. A referendum on each settlement was scheduled for 21 June 1989 to adopt the proposed Accord. However, concerns still existed relating to the powers of the General Council and the settlement councils and the accessibility of settlement membership to nonsettlement Metis. Nevertheless, the referendum was to go ahead as scheduled.[95]

In the June referendum, 77 percent of those who voted supported the agreement.[96] As a result, the Alberta-Metis Settlements Accord was executed by Premier Getty and Randy Hardy, President of the Federation, on 1 July 1989.[97] The agreement committed both parties to the implementation of its components and a mutually acceptable process to conclude the drafting of Metis settlements legislation. It also indicated that the Accord would resolve the litigation between the province and the Federation and any issues raised in it. The components of the Accord include: Resolution 18, Bills 64 and 65, a proposed agreement on financial assistance and resource management, an agreement to establish the Metis Settlements Transition Commission (a temporary body established to oversee the effective implementation of the Accord) and an agreement concerning the co-management of subsurface resources.

The greatest opposition to the Accord came from Paddle Prairie. In June, 78 percent of the members of Paddle Prairie who voted, voted in favour of the proposal. However, in a special meeting held on 14 November 1989, Paddle Prairie council voted to withdraw from the Federation. After studying the proposals, the council claimed that the Federation had ignored the concerns of Paddle Prairie in the negotiation process. In their opinion, title should vest in the settlements and policy-making power in the settlement councils. Further, they claimed, revenues generating from Paddle Prairie should be placed in their own trust fund. They were also concerned about the lack of detail on membership and land use issues. A referendum was held again in January 1990 in which 119 members voted against the council's decision to pull out and eighty-six voted in favour.[98]

Negotiations relating to the implementation of the Accord gave rise to the introduction of four new bills to the Legislative Assembly (33, 34, 35 and 36)[99] and subsequently the enactment of the *Metis Settlements Accord Implementation Act*, *Metis Settlements Land Protection Act*, *Metis Settlements Act* (*MSA*), and the *Constitution of Alberta Amendment Act*, 1990.[100]

# 3

# Overview of the
# 1990 Metis Settlements Legislation

## STRUCTURE AND AUTHORITY OF METIS GOVERNMENT

The new governing structure created by the legislation includes the establishment of a settlement corporation for each of the eight Metis settlements: Paddle Prairie, Peavine, Gift Lake, East Prairie, Buffalo Lake, Kikino, Elizabeth and Fishing Lake. Each settlement has the rights, powers and privileges of a natural person subject to a limited number of financial activities which require ministerial regulation or authorization by a settlement and the General Council (discussed below). Each settlement is governed by a settlement council composed of five councillors elected from the persons who are members of that settlement. Elections, resignations, disqualifications, delegation of authority, administrative structures, meeting and decision-making procedures are modelled on other provincial legislation and are dealt with in Part 1 of the *MSA*.

Each settlement council has powers analogous to those of a municipality, including the power to enact by-laws applicable within the geographic area of the settlement.[101] By-law authority includes the power to enact by-laws concerning matters of internal management, health, safety, welfare, public order, safety, fire protection, nuisance, pests, animals, airports, advertising, refuse disposal, parks, recreation, control of business, installation of water and sewage connections, sewerage fees, development levies, land use planning and development, and other miscellaneous matters.[102] By-laws must be given three separate readings at a meeting of the settlement council and, after the second reading, must be presented at a public meeting and approved by a majority vote of the settlement members present at the meeting.[103] Settlement councils also have authority to make decisions on membership and land allocation subject to appeal.[104] By-laws, membership and land allocation decisions must conform with provincial legislation and General Council Policy. Further, by-laws must be prepared in consultation with, and approved by, the Minister for the first three years after the *MSA* comes into force unless the Minister makes a regulation specifying the subject matter of by-laws that are exempt.[105]

The General Council is a representative corporate body composed of four elected officers and all of the settlement councillors. The powers of the General Council are also stipulated in the *MSA*.[106] The General Council has the authority to enact policies affecting the collective interests of the settlements in areas such as membership, land development, finance, hunting fishing and trapping. These policies require varying degrees of settlement approval depending on the subject matter of the policy, and must be published in the *Alberta Gazette* (Appendix 3). Policies are subject to ministerial veto, but the General Council may request the Minister make regulations specifying that particular policies, amendments or repeals are not subject to ministerial approval. General Council policies inconsistent with provincial legislation are of no effect to the extent of the inconsistency, unless otherwise provided by legislation. An exception are policies relating to hunting, trapping and gathering which are given priority over provincial legislation. However, these policies *must* be approved by all settlements and the Lieutenant Governor in Council.[107]

## THE METIS SETTLEMENTS APPEAL TRIBUNAL

The *MSA* also establishes the Metis Settlements Appeal Tribunal to hear appeals and references on matters of a local nature as required by legislation, settlement by-laws or General Council Policy. The Tribunal is a quasi-judicial body established to settle disputes relating to membership, land dealings, surface rights, and any other matter the parties involved agree to submit to the Tribunal's jurisdiction. Remedial powers of the Tribunal include the power to amend or repeal settlement by-laws, refer decisions back to the settlement council to be reconsidered, direct the Registrar of the Metis Settlements Land Registry to correct errors and omissions, confirm the substance of an agreement under an order of the Tribunal and any other remedy it deems appropriate in the circumstance. The desire to provide a nonadversarial alternative is maintained in the ability of the Appeal Tribunal to act as an arbitrator, to appoint an arbitrator, or to refer the dispute to a mediator. Decisions of the Appeal Tribunal may, with leave of the Alberta Court of Queen's Bench, be enforced in the same manner as a judgement or order of the Court. Appeals from a decision of the Appeal Tribunal on a question of law or jurisdiction may be made to the Alberta Court of Appeal.

The Appeal Tribunal is composed of a chairperson appointed by the Minister from a list provided by General Council, three members appointed by General Council, three members appointed by the Minister, and the remainder by agreement. The Chairperson is authorized to establish panels of three or more members of the Tribunal. If a panel is established to deal with membership issues, the majority of the panel must be appointed by the Minister. If a panel is established to deal with issues of land allocation, the majority of the members must be appointed by General Council. Two standing panels are also created by the legislation: the

Land Access Panel and the Existing Leases Land Access Panel. These panels are created to make decisions formerly within the jurisdiction of the Alberta Surface Rights Board.[108]

The Appeal Tribunal is currently in operation and as of April 1994 has issued twenty-one orders. The initial orders issued by the Tribunal illustrate an informal and flexible procedure suited to the needs of the particular parties and the broad scope of the Tribunal's fact finding and remedial powers. The first order issued on 28 November 1991 (*William Howse v. Glen Cardinal Sr. and Kikino Metis Settlement*) involved a contract dispute in which the claimant entered into a contract with a member of the Kikino Metis Settlement and the settlement to construct an addition to the member's residence. The value of the contract was $4,800 with payment to be received as work progressed. The claimant commenced construction and received two payments totalling $2,000. Prior to completion, the plaintiff was fired. The claimant alleged that he was entitled to another $1,400 for work completed before being removed from the project. All parties to the dispute agreed to the jurisdiction of the Appeal Tribunal and presented their arguments at an informal preliminary hearing at which all parties were present. Following the hearing, a panel of the Tribunal visited Kikino to view the construction at issue and to hold further discussions with the parties. After completing these investigations, the Appeal Tribunal rendered its decision. The Tribunal held that a valid contract was entered between the parties, that the work performed by the claimant would have been acceptable to all parties had he not been fired, and that the claimant was entitled to the $1,400 payment claimed.

The second order issued on 25 March 1992 (*Kikino Settlement Council v. Harrison Cardinal and Kib Hogenson*) concerned an application to determine ownership of a parcel of land located on Kikino Metis Settlement. The dispute centred on a parcel of land allocated to a settlement member, K. Hogenson, by the Kikino Settlement Council and approved by the Metis Development Branch in July 1983. Another member, Harrison Cardinal, claimed that approximately twenty-five acres of the parcel at issue belonged to him as part of his traditional hay meadow which he and/or his family had controlled for fifty years. The issue was further complicated by a settlement council resolution passed on 7 March 1986 approving an application for allotment of the hay meadow to Cardinal. All parties to the dispute asked the Appeal Tribunal to resolve the matter. An informal preliminary hearing was held at the settlement at which time the Tribunal heard from all parties. Following the hearing, the Tribunal directed staff to meet with individuals involved to see if a solution could be negotiated without the need of a further hearing. An agreement could not be reached so a formal hearing was scheduled. In addition to hearing from the parties, the Tribunal heard evidence from a number of witnesses concerning the use of hay meadows and the method for transferring interests in the hay meadows to members of the Kikino Settlement. The Tribunal found that traditional hay meadows had once been governed by a permit system, but this was replaced by an application for quarter sections of land on which hay meadows were located. The quarter section at issue had been allocated as a unit to Hogenson and there was no evidence to suggest that the quarter section should not remain intact.

Two collateral issues addressed by the Tribunal were Wayne Cardinal's entitlement to compensation for improvements to the hay meadow and ownership of hay taken from the meadow by K. Hogenson. The Tribunal ordered that Kikino Settlement Council determine Wayne Cardinal's entitlement to compensation as there was no evidence as to the value of the improvements. Such compensation was directed to be paid by the settlement because Wayne Cardinal made the improvements in the belief that Harrison Cardinal had a right to the hay meadow as a result of the 1986 Settlement Council resolution. The Tribunal found the resolution was made in error. On the second issue, K. Hogenson was ordered to pay compensation to Wayne Cardinal for two-thirds of the hay bales removed. The rationale given was Hogenson did not prepare the land, seed it or take part in the haying of it. The standard practice in Kikino was to pay for land rental by giving one-third of the crop as payment. Hogenson would only be entitled to one-third of the bales if standard practice had been followed.

To date, only one decision of the Tribunal has been appealed to the Alberta Court of Appeal. The appeal indicates a reluctance to accept the broad jurisdiction asserted by the Tribunal in matters the Tribunal considers to be in the collective interest of settlement members. One of the issues on appeal was the jurisdiction of the Tribunal to hear an appeal to a subdivision and lease approval by a settlement member, Mr. C. Anderson, who was not "directly affected" by the approvals. Following s.8.1 of the Land Policy (which provides that the Appeal Tribunal can hear an appeal by *any person affected* by a decision of General Council or a Settlement Council) the Tribunal heard Mr. Anderson's appeal and stated: "Settlement lands are for the benefit and use of all the people of the community and any decision affecting these lands in turn affect the people living there." In its decision the Alberta Court of Appeal stated that "it is an abrogation of responsibility by the Tribunal to make a blanket statement that all members of the settlement who live there are directly affected." The Tribunal must look to "each case to decide if an appellant is truly 'directly affected'." (*R. Anderson v. Metis Settlement Appeal Tribunal and Clayton Anderson*, Nov. 4 and 5, Alta C.A. (unreported)). The matter was remitted back to the Tribunal which concluded that C. Anderson was not directly affected by the subdivision and therefore did not have status to launch an appeal (*Clayton Anderson and the Metis Settlements Subdivision Approving Authority and Randy Anderson Owner*, Order No. 17, January 26, 1994 and *Clayton Anderson and Randy Anderson and the Gift Lake Metis Settlement Council*, Order No. 18, January 26, 1994).

## MEMBERSHIP

Pursuant to the legislation, a Transitional Membership Regulation was enacted for the purpose of clarifying settlement membership as of 1 November 1990.[109] This regulation requires that each settlement council and the Minister provide the Commissioner of the Metis Settlements Transition Commission with a list of settlement members. Those people whose names appear on both lists are confirmed as members and those whose names appear on only one list are classified as uncertain members. Those who are declared to have uncertain status have the right to apply to the Appeal Tribunal for confirmation of membership.[110]

Other membership issues and rights of residency are addressed in the *MSA*.[111] Settlement councils are given the authority to accept or reject applications for membership subject to specified conditions relating to age, residence and proof of Metis identity. Metis persons are identified as people of aboriginal ancestry who identify with Metis history and culture.[112] A person registered as an Indian under the *Indian Act* or as a Inuk for the purposes of a land claim, is not eligible to apply for membership unless he or she was registered when less than 18 years old, lived a substantial part of his or her childhood in the settlement area, one or both of his or her parents are (or were) settlement members and membership is approved by a settlement by-law.[113] Settlement councils also have the authority to terminate memberships and to allocate land to settlement members subject to appeal to the Appeal Tribunal. Several conditions on membership, leaves of absence, residency and termination are specified in the legislation. Further, rights of residency are recognized in specified nonmembers such as immediate family of settlement members, teachers, health care workers and employees of the settlements.

## LAND INTERESTS AND LAND MANAGEMENT

Fee simple title to Metis lands is issued to General Council by way of letters patent.[114] The *Metis Settlements Land Protection Act* confirms the terms of the grant, places limits on disposition, and prohibits the use of settlement lands as security. Title to water and subsurface resources is retained by the province, but entry on settlement lands is prohibited without the consent of the affected settlement council in accordance with the terms of a Co-Management Agreement appended as Schedule 3 to the *MSA*. The Co-Management Agreement addresses issues of access, compatibility of development schemes with Metis land use, the establishment of a Metis Settlements Access Committee with powers to deny or set conditions of access, and Metis economic development rights. Specific procedures relating to acquiring rights of entry, terminating rights of entry, hearings, appeals, compensation, damages and reviews of compensation are set out in the *MSA*.[115]

Under the *MSA*, the only rights and interests in settlement land are those created by the Act, General Council Policy or settlement by-laws.[116] The Act also enables General Council to make policies in consultation with the Minister concerning a number of land-related matters including the creation, termination, disposition, and devolution of interests in settlement lands.[117] General Council has prepared a Land Policy.[118] The purpose of the Policy is to provide a basic system of interests in settlement land, establish principles governing the creation and transfer of those interests, and to create a land management system that balances the collective rights of the settlement with the individual rights of the landholder.[119] The Land Policy creates three distinct Metis interests in settlement land: Metis title (held by the settlement or settlement members), provisional Metis title, and allotments (discussed below). The Land Policy also provides for the creation and transfer of lesser interests such as easements, leases and licenses to settlement and nonsettlement members. The Land Interests Conversion Regulation has also been promulgated by the Minister to provide for the conversion and registration of interests held by settlement members under the *Metis Betterment Act*.[120]

The *Land Titles Act* does not apply to land in the settlement area.[121] In its place the Minister has made regulations regarding the establishment and operation of a Metis Settlements Land Registry (Metis Land Registry), the settlement of disputes arising from the Metis Settlements Land Registry Regulation (Registry Regulation) and the application of provincial land titles law.[122] The Registry Regulation is modelled on the recommendations of the joint provincial land titles committee for a model land recording and registration act.[123] Matters addressed in the Regulation include establishment of the Registry, recording, registration, interests overriding the register, compensation, powers of the Appeal Tribunal and courts, administration, procedures, document requirements, plans, interests passing on death, and adoption of some provisions of the *Land Titles Act*.

## FINANCIAL MATTERS

The *MSA* creates a two-part Consolidated Fund to be administered by the General Council. The legislation details the payment into the consolidated funds for specified purposes and requires the General Council to make a financial allocation policy. The main source of payment into the fund are surface revenues, money resulting from co-management of sub-surface resource agreements payable to the General Council and payments made from the Transition Fund established under the *Metis Settlements Accord Implementation Act*. In essence, the General Council assumes the role of trustee for money collected for the benefit of settlement lands, a role formerly assumed by the provincial government. The Act also provides for the establishment and protection of individual settlement funds, settlement funds and a consolidated fund.

## IMPLEMENTATION

The *Metis Settlements Accord Implementation Act* creates the Metis Settlements Transition Commission as a temporary mechanism for the implementation of the *MSA*. The Transition Commission is established as a corporation. A transitional authority composed of a Commissioner and two other members gives overall policy guidance. One member is appointed by General Council and one by the Lieutenant Governor in Council. The Commissioner is appointed by cabinet on recommendation from the other two appointees. The Transition Commission has the power to employ administrative and professional staff.[124] The Transition Commission automatically dissolves at the expiration of seven years unless otherwise agreed to by the Minister and General Council. The Commissioner has broad powers and responsibilities including the management and control of finances, administration and provision of services of government programs, initiation of programs to implement the legislation, and assisting settlement councils in the assumption of their governing powers. The Transition Authority is directly accountable to both the General Council and the Minister. The Commissioner's activities are monitored through the Transition Authority, annual reports tabled in the Alberta Legislative Assembly, annual audits and judicial review.

The Act also establishes a Transition Fund and schedule of payments to assist in the implementation of self-government. Transitional funding is provided through annual conditional grants of $25 million over a period of seven years to be used for capital projects, operations and maintenance (for example, administration, protective services, environment, utilities, community service, land development, transportation, housing). The annual sum of $5 million is also to held by the Commissioner or deposited in Part 2 of the Consolidated Fund over a term of seven years. The fund is administered by the General Council for the benefit of settlements and their members.[125] The General Council is also to be paid annual payments of $10 million a year over a period of ten years for the benefit of the settlement and its members. In total, the transitional financing amounts to the payment of $310 million for the benefit of the Metis over a period of seventeen years. At the expiration of seventeen years, it is hoped that "the Settlements will have developed economically to the point where they will function financially in the same way as other local governments."[126]

Finally, the Act also stays the natural resources trust fund litigation arising from administration of trust funds under former legislation. It also extinguishes future litigation arising from the former legislation or the province's fiduciary obligation to Metis peoples.[127]

## CONSTITUTIONAL AMENDMENT

The new legislation adopts several methods to protect the Metis land base including restrictions on disposition, restrictions on the taking of security interests in settlement lands and limitations on the province's right to expropriate settlement lands. The most significant step in the protection of Metis land is the *Constitution of Alberta Amendment Act, 1990* which confirms the details of the Metis land grant, including limits placed on expropriation and seizure, in the Alberta constitution.[128] The Act prohibits the Legislature from amending or repealing the *Metis Settlements Land Protection Act*, revoking letters patent granting settlement land to the General Council, and dissolving General Council or changing its composition without agreement of the General Council. The constitutional amendment cannot be repealed by the Legislature until such time as Metis settlement land is protected by the Canadian constitution — a proposal the federal government so far has refused to act on.

# 4  Descriptive Overview of the Metis Settlements Land Registry

## PURPOSES AND APPLICATION

The basic purposes of the Metis Settlements Land Registry, like any system of interest recording and title registration, are to provide for certainty of ownership in land, simplify proof of ownership, facilitate economic and efficient disposition of interests in land, and provide compensation for persons who sustain loss through unauthorized registrations.[129] The creation of a separate Registry located in the settlement area promotes local monitoring and control over the creation of interests in, and development of, settlement lands; easy access to settlement and settlement members; the creation of a registry system which reflects the unique interests held in Metis lands; and, a mechanism for recording interests, developing recording instruments and providing remedies consistent with the concept of collective ownership of the settlement area. Although a combined government/Metis initiative, the Registry is intended to enable Metis peoples to monitor the transfer of interests in their own land through the appointment of a registrar and local staff and advisors considered necessary for the operation of the Registry.[130]

The creation of a unique registry system has the potential of hindering commercial development if developers cannot be assured of the nature and priority of the interests which they acquire. Further complications and distrust could arise through the creation of unfamiliar recording and registration systems, dispute resolution mechanisms and legal documentation of land transactions.[131] It is likely that these problems inherent in other unique registry systems, such as the Indian Land Register, will be preempted by the enactment of the Registry Regulation which closely resembles the provincial land titles system.[132] The proposed Registry Regulation is modelled on recommendations for a *Model Land Recording and Registration Act* for all provinces and the territories.[133] Although it contains slight variations to accommodate the unique land interests of the General Council, settlements and settlement members, provisions affecting interests of nonsettlement members envisage the recording and registration of interests created by contract, postponement, transfer and other familiar legal means. The system contemplated not only provides a means of giving public notice of legal interests in settlement lands, but also provides a guarantee of entitlement, compensation for those who sustain loss through the Registrar's error, and recourse to the Appeal Tribunal or Court of Queen's Bench. Overriding interests, interests existing prior to the enactment of the settlements legislation and priority of recorded and registered interests are also addressed. Consequently, like the provincial land titles system, the Metis system will allow an efficient and accurate interpretation of the registry record. This is of crucial importance as Metis lands are pulled completely out of the provincial land titles system and the *Land Titles Act* will not apply to land in the settlement area except to the limited extent it has been incorporated in the Registry Regulation.[134]

## GENERAL DESCRIPTION OF THE REGISTRY SYSTEM

There are two fundamental elements to the system: the administrative element, which is a comprehensive system for compiling records which disclose all interests in the settlement lands; and the legal element which confers title, provides security of ownership, facilitates transfer of interests in land and establishes interest priorities through a system of recording and registration of interests in land.[135] General Council Policy, Metis settlements legislation, settlement by-laws and other provincial legislation determine what documents and interests can be recorded or registered. Recording and registration refer to the administrative process through which entries on a register secure priority of interests in land, and in the case of registration, also confirm or terminate the interest. The effect of recording is to confer a priority of the recorded interest *vis-à-vis* other recorded interests. The effect of registration is to confirm both priority and ownership. Priority conferred is subject only to overriding interests and the equitable jurisdiction of the court.[136]

Interest recording and registration assumes the creation of registers. Under the Registry Regulation, three categories of registers are created: fee simple registers, Metis title registers and interest registers. The fee simple register is issued in the name of the General Council. The Metis title registers are established for each unit of land held by way of Metis title. Interest registers may be created for units of land held other than by way of fee simple or Metis title (for example, provisional Metis title and allotments).[137] Each register will contain a description of the types of interest for which the register is created and the legal description of the parcel (unit of land) for which there is an interest in the register; the name of the registered owner; the date transfers of interests are recorded and "identifiers" of various matters such as previous registers, documents which register, transfer, or terminate interests, and recorded interests which purport to affect a registered interest.[138]

All interests in land created by the settlements legislation, General

Council Policy, settlement by-laws, and other provincial laws not re-pealed or amended by the settlements legislation or regulations may be recorded in the appropriate register.[139] The interest is recorded by sub-mitting an original document, or copy of a document on which the inter-est is based, or a document summarizing the transaction on which the interest is based.[140] Upon submission of the document, the Registrar must enter an identifier of the document in the register established for the unit of land affected. Special procedures are also outlined for the filing of plans of survey and descriptive plans required by the Registrar before re-cording any interest.[141] Again, it must be repeated that recording does not confer or confirm the existence, nature or ownership of the interest. The effect of recording is to give notice of the interest and to determine priori-ties as against others who may record an interest against the same parcel of land.

Subject to a few exceptions relating to interests created prior to the en-actment of the settlements legislation, priority is conferred in accordance with the date of recording. Generally, an earlier interest is to be enforced with priority over a later conflicting interest. Priority is maintained in successors to the interest from the date of the recording of the original in-terest.[142] Under certain circumstances, the Registrar may cancel the re-cording of an interest. However, this will not terminate the interest or its priority. Rather, a valid interest can only be terminated by process of law including an order by the Appeal Tribunal or the Court of Queen's Bench.[143]

Unlike recording, the registration of an interest in the appropriate reg-ister confers both priorities and title. A registered owner will be deemed the owner of the interest, whether or not ownership would have been recognized at common law, if the interest is qualified for registration, the registered owner has the legal capacity to hold the interest and, in the case of Metis title, provisional Metis title and allotments, the owner is the settlement or settlement member in the area the land is located.[144] The Registry Regulation identifies interests which qualify for registration. These include the fee simple, Metis title, provisional Metis title, allot-ments, and other interests authorized by General Council Policy, such as leaseholds, easements and covenants.[145] The Registry Regulation also out-lines the circumstances under which a registration can be revised or can-celled including cases of fraud and interests arising from invalid transactions. If a registration is cancelled, it will terminate the interest re-corded. Where persons are prejudiced by unauthorized registrations aris-ing from invalid transactions, application can be made to the Appeal Tribunal or Court for a declaration of the rights of the parties, orders for revision of the registration and compensation.[146]

In theory, the register is supposed to reflect all interests and priorities in relation to a particular piece of land. However, like other registry systems, the Registry Regulation recognizes that the system must admit the priority of certain interests which are neither recorded or registered. These interests are discussed in further detail later in this book.

The Registry Regulation also anticipates compensating people who suffer as a result of a malfunctioning of the system. It establishes an assurance fund for the payment of compensation and the circumstances pursuant to which payments can be made from the fund. It also specifies the grounds for entitlement to compensation from the Registrar, the amount of compensation, the power of the Registrar to enter compensation agreements, time limits within which compensation claims must be made, and circumstances under which a person may apply to the Appeal Tribunal or court for a compensation order.[147]

One of the more unique aspects of the Registry Regulation is the process provided for the resolution of disputes. Disputes arising from the application of land titles law are normally within the jurisdiction of the Court of Queen's Bench. Part 7 of the Registry Regulation allows aggrieved persons and the Registrar to apply to the Appeal Tribunal or the courts for the resolution of disputes. In any proceeding before the Appeal Tribunal, the Tribunal may give any order it thinks proper including directing the Registrar to record an interest, cancel a recording, register an interest or revise a registration. Unless a judgement, order or certificate which cancels or terminates interests states otherwise, it may only be registered if it is consented to by the parties or their lawyers, was granted *ex parte* and states it need not be served on anyone, and is accompanied by an undertaking that an appeal will not be sought (or the time for appeal has expired).[148] There is some argument concerning the constitutional validity of the Appeal Tribunal because it exercises functions normally exercised by a court. It is hoped that this problem is addressed in s.53 of the Registry Regulation which provides:

> In any proceeding in the Court of Queen's Bench for the determination of rights of the parties to the proceeding, that court has all of the powers of the Appeal Tribunal under this Regulation.[149]

Finally, it should be noted that several provisions of the *Land Titles Act* have been adopted. Some of the more significant provisions include implied terms that a transferor will do all acts necessary to give effect to transfer documents, implied terms in documents conveying interests subject to a security interest that monies owing under the security will be paid, grant of restrictive covenants or easements to oneself, registration of partywall and encroachment agreements, consent for surrender of registered leases and recording of writs of execution and interests of execution creditors.[150]

# 5   <u>Rights and Interests in Settlement Lands</u>

## Application of Common Law

Section 99 of the *MSA* provides that a right or interest in settlement lands may exist only under the *MSA*, another act, General Council Policy or settlement by-laws. Although the section does not expressly contemplate the recognition of rights or interests arising by operation of the common law, principles of common law may be applied in the resolution of disputes and interpretation of rights, unless they are expressly excluded by, or are inconsistent with, the provisions or purpose of the Act, General Council Policy or settlement by-laws.[151] Some difficulty will be encountered in the application of common law principles to unique interests created by the Land Policy, such as Metis title. Because the interest is unique, there are no existing common law rules governing the interpretation of rights associated with this interest. In the absence of clear direction from the Land Policy, legislation or settlement by-laws, the Appeal Tribunal or Court of Appeal may search for and create analogous common law rules to resolve disputes.

## Application of Equity

Historically, rules of common law were administered in a relatively inflexible manner and the remedies for the enforcement of rights under common law were limited. As a result, a system of justice called equity evolved which was founded on the principle that "its remedies were discretionary and would evolve to suit the justice required for new situations."[152] Principles of equity may apply to enhance or limit rights in land. For centuries two distinct court systems existed in England which administered common law and equity respectively. Today, both law and equity are administered by Canadian courts. Unless principles of equity are expressly abolished, they may operate to alter rights and interests created by legislation, Land Policy and settlement by-laws.[153] Equitable doctrines resulting in the recognition of equitable interests in land are enforceable and need not be registered.

## Application of Provincial Law

Section 222 of the *MSA* enables General Council, after consultation with the Minister, to make policies respecting the creation, termination, disposition, and devolution of interests in settlement lands. General Council also has the authority to place reservations, exceptions, conditions and limitations on entitlement to rights or interests. These powers are broad enough to allow the creation of a unique system of landholding which may or may not include the application of common law and equity. However, in absence of express statutory authority, ministerial regulation or consequential amendments or repeal of conflicting provincial legislation, General Council does not have the authority to exclude the application of provincial legislation. As a result, provisions in the Land Policy which conflict with provincial legislation are likely unenforceable. Support for this conclusion is drawn from the following observations:

1. Section 99 of the *MSA* recognizes rights and interests which exist under the *MSA* "or another Act."

2. Where General Council Policy is able to override provincial legislation, this right has been explicitly granted (for example, s.222(1)(v) enables the General Council to exclude the application of the *Administration of Estates Act*, the *Devolution of Real Property Act*, and the *Wills Act*).[154]

3. Section 230 of the *MSA* states that General Council Policies which are inconsistent with the *MSA* "or any other enactment" are of no effect to the extent of the inconsistency unless the *MSA*, or any other enactment, otherwise provides.

4. Sections 239 and 242 of the *MSA* anticipate the resolution of difficulties arising from the application of other legislation through regulations enacted at the request of the General Council.

5. Part 13 of the *MSA* specifies consequential amendments to and the repeal of legislation which has the potential of conflicting with the settlements legislation.

As discussed below, this issue is relevant in determining the application of legislated provincial land law such as the *Water Resources Act, Limitation of Actions Act, Landlord and Tenant Act, Public Lands Act, Dower Act, Matrimonial Property Act, Intestate Succession Act*, and *Ultimate Heir Act*.[155]

## INTEREST OF THE GENERAL COUNCIL IN PATENTED LANDS

The fee simple estate is the largest estate known in law. The word "fee" indicates an estate of inheritance and the word "simple" indicates that descent on death is not limited to a particular heir, but may pass to ascendants, descendants, lineals or collaterals. In short, "fee simple" means the estate while describing its two essential elements: potential infinite duration and inheritability by collateral and lineal descendants. The estate ends only when its holder dies intestate without leaving heirs as defined in the *Intestate Succession Act*. In Alberta, if there are no heirs entitled by law to the estate, or they fail to claim the estate within a specified time, the estate escheats to the Crown in the right of Alberta pursuant to the *Ultimate Heir Act*. Other elements traditionally associated with ownership of a fee simple are the rights of use, enjoyment, profit, management, alienation and devise. The fee simple may be granted subject to condition in which case the fee simple is not a fee simple "absolute," but depending upon the nature of the condition, a conditional or determinable fee.

Fee simple title to all of the Metis settlements has been issued to the General Council by way of letters patent. The fee simple title is subject to reservations from title set out in the letters patent and the *Metis Settlements Land Protection Act*.[156] Mines and minerals, water, fixtures and improvements placed by the Crown prior to the grant, and palaeontological and archaeological resources and interests acquired prior to the grant are reserved from title. The Crown also reserves specific rights of user such as the right of diversion and use of water, the right to work mines and minerals, the right to manage highways and roads constructed prior to the grant, the right of fishery and the right of access to Crown fixtures and improvements.

The letters patent and *Metis Settlements Land Protection Act* also place conditions on General Council's title which operate to restrict the rights of the General Council and protect the Metis land base. The patented lands cannot be alienated without consent of all the settlements and the majority of settlement members. Rights of the Crown upon the breach of this condition are not specified. However, under common law, the Crown retains a right of re-entry; that is, the right to resume title. The letters patent and legislation also prohibit using patented lands as security for debt. Security given or taken contrary to this condition is void (that is, has no legal force or binding effect). The patented land is also protected by conditions placed on the Crown's power of expropriation and conditions for entry. The lands cannot be expropriated without the agreement of General Council and payment of compensation. If no agreement can be reached, the matter is to be determined by the Court of Queen's Bench. Even though title to subsurface resources remains with the Crown, entry to the settlement lands for the purpose of exploration and development is prohibited without consent of the affected settlement council and the General Council in accordance with provisions of the Co-Management Agreement.

## Land Interest Conversion

The Land Interests Conversion Regulation creates a process for reviewing and converting pre-existing land allocations granted to settlement members under the former *Metis Betterment Act*.[157] Settlement members who hold an allocation when the regulation comes into force, or successors in title to the member, may apply to have their interests converted to interests created under the General Council Land Policy. These interests are Metis title, provisional Metis title and memoranda of allotment. Metis title is the largest and most secure interest a settlement member can hold in settlement lands. The amount of land that can be held by Metis title is limited. However, a member can hold additional lands for a fixed term by memorandum of allotment. Allotments may only be granted for the purpose of operating a farm, ranch or business. The Land Policy also stipulates conditions that must be met before Metis title will be issued. However, an interest in land called provisional Metis title may be granted for a fixed term by members who wish to use and make necessary improvements required for the issuance of Metis title.

Application for conversion is made to the settlement council in whose area the land allocation is located. Pre-existing allocations are extinguished when the allocation is converted under the regulation, a new interest is recorded in the Land Registry and all rights of appeal are over. These interests will also be extinguished if a holder ceases to be a settlement member or application is not made for conversion on or before 30 June 1995.[158] Council must decide whether or not to approve an application within ninety days after the application is received. Appeals from the decision of the settlement council may be made to the Appeal Tribunal.

The Land Policy and Registry Regulation provide for the automatic recording of certificates of occupancy and other pre-existing interests held by settlement members, or successors in title ("interim allocations") in the Metis Land Registry.[159] The legal effect of recording is to confer priorities *vis-à-vis* other recorded interests based on the time of recording. Recorded interim allocations may only be extinguished or converted to new interests in accordance with the Land Interests Conversion Regulation. Upon conversion, pre-existing interests may be registered. Unlike recording, registration confers and confirms both priorities based on the time of recording and ownership of the interest as defined in the register. Once converted, the effective date for determining priorities is the date the interest was created when the original interest was granted under the former Act.[160]

Pre-existing interests held by nonsettlement members are also recognized under the new system.[161] Pre-existing nonmember interests such as easements, covenants, rights of removal, and leases may be recorded, but not registered, in the Metis Settlements Land Registry. If recorded on or before 30 June 1993, these interests cannot be refused for noncompliance with the Registry Regulation or Registrar's rules and will be enforced with priority over other interests recorded prior to the pre-existing interests.[162] Pre-existing interests become registerable interests, thereby confirming both priority and ownership, only if they are authorized to be registered by General Council Policy. Disputes relating to the recording or registration of these interests may be raised before the Appeal Tribunal and the Court of Queen's Bench. Special authorization procedures apply to rights of access and removal by parties who held mineral rights at the time the legislation came into force or who fall within the definition of an "operator" under the *MSA*. These procedures are discussed in further detail below.

## Metis Title

Metis title in each of the eight settlement areas is held by the corresponding settlement corporation created under the *MSA* unless it is registered in the name of a settlement member. In the event a person who is not entitled to hold Metis title is registered as holder in the Metis Land Registry, the settlement holds Metis title in trust for whomever the law determines should hold it.[163] The policy contemplates that Metis title will be acquired through conversion of pre-existing interests, inheritance from deceased settlement members or application to the settlement by holders of provisional Metis title and allotments. Acquisition from other settlement members is implied, but not explicitly addressed. The settlement *must* approve the transfer of Metis title to holders of provisional title and allotments if certain conditions stipulated in the Land Policy are met. Metis title is described in s.2.4 of the Land Policy as follows:

2.4 Nature of Metis Title

(1) Subject to this Policy and settlement by-laws, the holder of the Metis title in a parcel has the exclusive right:

    (a) to use and occupy the land;
    (b) to make improvements to the land;
    (c) to transfer the Metis title;
    (d) to grant lesser interests as set out in this Policy; and
    (e) to determine who receives Metis title on the holder's death.

(2) The holder of the Metis title also has any additional rights with respect to the parcel that are specifically provided for by General Council Policy or any other enactment.

(3) The Metis title is subject to the following interests whether or not they are registered:

   (a) natural rights of air, water and support;
   (b) traditional community pathways and uses.

(4) In order to clarify traditional community pathways and uses a settlement can pass a by-law locating and describing them for settlement held land.[164]

The rights attributed to the holder of Metis title are rights traditionally associated with owners of a fee simple estate. For example, Metis title is inheritable and is of infinite duration. However, it is most similar to a conditional fee because conditions and limitations are placed on acquisition and disposition. For example, individuals must be members of the settlement in order to obtain Metis title, limitations are placed on the amount of land held by individual settlement members, the creation of lesser interests must be approved by settlement council, and lands held by settlement members cannot be given as security except in accordance with General Council Policy.[165]

Despite these similarities, Metis title is more accurately perceived as a unique statutory interest which is less than the fee simple estate. Several arguments can be made to support this interpretation. First, the Land Policy does not adopt language traditionally associated with the creation and identification of a fee simple, but adopts a new phrase, "Metis title." Second, it is clear from the settlements legislation and the Registry Regulation that a single fee simple interest is held in the patented land by the General Council.[166] Third, the Land Policy and settlement legislation do not explicitly create rights of re-entry upon conditions broken. Although this is not essential to create a conditional fee at common law, it helps clarify the nature of the estate created. Finally, the inapplicability of the *Wills Act*, unique rules governing the devolution of Metis title on death of the holder, the apparent inapplicability of the *Ultimate Heir Act*, restrictions placed on disposition, and the condition that Metis title can only be held by the settlement or a settlement member, suggest that Metis title is a new and unique interest that merely looks like a conditional fee.

Although a unique interest has been created, analogous principles of common law may be applied in the resolution of disputes if the Land Policy, settlement by-laws or legislation fail to address the legal effect of broken conditions. Rights implied will vary depending on the classification of the condition at issue. A condition may be similar to a condition precedent, subsequent or both a condition precedent and subsequent. A condition precedent is a condition of acquisition. If the condition is not met, title does not pass from the grantor to the grantee. If the condition is a condition subsequent the interest will pass to the grantee subject to compliance with the condition. If the condition is broken the grantor may exercise a right of re-entry and reclaim the interest as her own. For example, an individual must be a settlement member to receive and register Metis title. This condition is similar to a condition precedent. If the condition is not met, Metis title cannot be transferred. Alternatively, if a person was a member but ceases to be a member, the condition may operate as a condition subsequent giving rise to a right of re-entry in the settlement.

## Provisional Metis Title

The description of provisional Metis title is contained in s.2.5 of the Land Policy and the Memorandum of Provisional Metis Title attached to the Policy. Section 2.5 describes provisional Metis title as follows:

2.5 Nature of Provisional Metis Title

(1) The Settlement Council can grant a settlement member provisional Metis title in settlement held land to enable the member to use the land and make improvements to the extent needed to obtain Metis title.

(2) A provisional Metis title can only be granted in land for which the settlement holds the Metis title.

(3) The provisional Metis title in a parcel in a settlement area can only be held by the settlement, or someone who is a member of the settlement and has signed a Memorandum of Provisional Metis Title for the parcel.

(4) A Memorandum of Provisional Metis Title must state

    (a) the conditions, including improvements to be made to the land, which if met will give the holder the right to acquire the Metis title;

    (b) how much time the holder has to satisfy the conditions and what rights of renewal, if any, there are if the conditions are not met in time;

    (c) what rights and duties the holder has with respect to the land; and

    (d) any other matters that are specified by settlement by-law, regulation or General Council Policy.

(5) A Memorandum of Provisional Metis Title must be in the form attached to this Policy.

(6) Subject to this Policy, settlement by-laws, and the terms of the Memorandum, the holder of the provisional Metis title in a parcel has the exclusive right to use and occupy the land for the purpose of improving the land as required to obtain Metis title.[167]

Provisional Metis title confers a right of exclusive use and occupation to a settlement member for a fixed term of five years (subject to renewal for another five years). Procedures for granting provisional Metis title and considerations relevant to the grant are specified in the Land Policy. When settlement council determines that land is to be made available for this purpose, it must provide public notice of availability of the interest, the application requirements and its decision. Certain conditions relating to acquisition, retention of the interest and qualification for Metis title are also specified in the Land Policy and Memorandum of Provisional Metis Title. Upon these conditions being met, a settlement member may apply to the settlement council for Metis title to the lands held by way of provisional title.[168]

Provisional Metis title most closely resembles a fixed-term lease which is characterized by the retention of a reversionary interest in the landlord and a grant of exclusive possession to the tenant for a fixed period of time. Although the obligation to pay rent was once considered an integral aspect of a tenancy relationship, this is no longer the case. Therefore, the fact that members do not pay rent for provisional Metis title is insufficient to take this relationship out of the category of a common law tenancy. The most important element of a tenancy is the grant of exclusive possession. The holder of provisional Metis title has the exclusive right to use and occupy the land for the purpose of improving the land as required to obtain Metis title. Despite these similarities, the relationship between the settlement and holder of provisional Metis title may not be a tenancy. Granting of exclusive possession is a question of substance, not form. The issue of exclusivity is determined by looking at the actual relationship between the landlord and tenant, not the labels and words in a document. If a settlement member does not have actual exclusive possession, the relationship created may be more similar to a contractual license.

Both the Land Policy and Registry Regulation distinguish between provisional Metis title, leases and licenses. This suggests that General Council is attempting to create a unique legal relationship between the settlement and settlement members. However, as defined, provisional Metis title is a leasehold interest.[169] Failure to identify all rights and conditions in unambiguous terms may result in the application of analogous principles of common law in the determination of rights. For example, the right of the settlement upon the expiration of the term of provisional Metis title is not specified. Application of analogous principles suggests that the settlement retains a reversionary interest in the land as holder of Metis title. As provisional Metis title is granted for a fixed term, the tenancy will automatically end at the expiration of the period stipulated. At this point the land is no longer encumbered by the tenancy and the settlement is free to resume physical possession.[170]

Analogous principles of common law may also be applied to determine rights of the settlement and settlement members on conditions broken. Conditions stated in the Land Policy and Memorandum of Provisional Metis Title are clearly intended to address the legal competency of the recipient, the retention of the holder's interest, and conditions which must be met in order to acquire Metis title. Provisional Metis title may only be held by a settlement or settlement member and will only be granted if a Memorandum of Provisional Metis Title has been signed. The consequences of failing to meet these conditions is not stated. However, the most logical interpretation is that the tenancy-like relationship is not created and an interest in land does not pass to the settlement or settlement member.

The Memorandum of Provisional Metis Title also identifies conditions which, if broken, give rise to a right of termination by written notice from the settlement. Further conditions may be imposed by settlement by-law, regulation or General Council Policy. Sixty days after the settlement has given written notice, provisional title is ended. The land must be returned to the settlement within a further sixty days unless an appeal to the Appeal Tribunal is pending. There is also a possibility that improvements to the land will become the property of the settlement. The rights retained by the settlement are very similar to those found in many leases which allow a landlord to re-enter land and forfeit the lease where the tenant has breached certain terms. Given the severity of this remedy, conditions giving rise to this right are normally construed very strictly against the landlord. Further, the exercise of the landlord's rights is qualified by the Court's discretion to grant equitable relief against forfeiture.[171] A similar discretion could be exercised by the Appeal Tribunal.

### Allotment

As discussed earlier, the amount of land a person may hold under Metis title is limited. However, a settlement council can grant a member additional lands by memorandum of allotment for a fixed period of time for specified purposes such as farming, ranching or operating a business. Procedures and factors to be considered in the acquisition of allotments are outlined in the Land Policy and the Memorandum of Allotment attached to it.[172] The nature of an allotment is most similar to a leasehold interest at common law and is described in s.2.6 of the Land Policy as follows:

2.6 Nature of an allotment

(1) A settlement can grant an allotment in settlement held land to a member to operate a farm, ranch or business.

(2) An allotment can only be granted in land for which the settlement holds the Metis title.

(3) An allotment in a parcel in a settlement area can only be held by the

settlement, or someone who is a member of the settlement and has signed a Memorandum of Allotment for the parcel.

(4) A Memorandum of Allotment must state

    (a) the period of time for which the allotment is granted;

    (b) the allotment holder's rights of renewal, if any;

    (c) the rights and duties of the allotment holder with respect to the land; and

    (d) any other matters that are specified by settlement by-law, regulation or General Council Policy.

(5) A Memorandum of Allotment must be in the form attached to this Policy.

(6) Subject to this Policy, settlement by-laws, and the terms of the Memorandum, the holder of an allotment has the exclusive right to use and occupy the land.[173]

The same arguments concerning the creation of a tenancy relationship and the potential effects of creating a tenancy by way of provisional Metis title apply to allotments. Many of the conditions associated with allotments are identical to those associated with provisional title.

### Limitations on Metis Title, Provisional Metis Title and Allotments

Several conditions and limitations are placed on the acquisition and disposition of member-held land and the creation of lesser interests. Some of the more significant limitations include:

1. Metis title held by a member is limited to one hamlet lot and a total area of 175 acres. Metis title may be issued for an additional 167 acres if such land is used and required for the operation of a farm, ranch or business.[174] The settlement council cannot grant Metis title in excess of these limitations. If Metis title is received in excess of this amount, it is held by the settlement in trust for the person the law determines it should be held for. If analogous common law principles are applied, title may remain in the original grantor of the interest.

2. The settlement must approve a transfer of Metis title from the settlement and interests acquired as the result of a member's death to a holder of provisional Metis title or allotment if the applicant is a member who is living in the settlement; has no overdue debts to the settlement; is living on the land or operating a farm, business or ranch on it; has made improvements to the land stipulated in the Land Policy; and the transfer would not exceed land holding limits.[175] Each of these is analogous to a condition precedent and must be met prior to the transfer of Metis title. A settlement may, by by-law, establish additional conditions of acquisition.

3. The holder of Metis title can lease lands to anyone but leases to

nonsettlement members must be approved by the settlement council. Leases exceeding ten years must be approved by by-law.[176]

4. Licenses, covenants, easements, and utility rights of way in member-held land can not be granted without approval of settlement council. Where such interests granted by the settlement in settlement-held land, or an individual in member-held land, exceed ten years, they are of no effect unless approved by settlement by-law.[177]

5. Land held by a settlement member may not be given as security except in accordance with the Land Policy. Security given or taken contrary to this prohibition is void. The Land Policy does not provide for the granting of security in settlement- or member-held lands but clearly recognizes the potential existence of charges against interests of non-members.[178]

6. Metis title, provisional Metis title and allotments cannot be held by more than one person at a time. A note to the policy explains this reference is to tenants in common and joint tenants. Transfers that contravene this prohibition are void.[179] As drafted, the prohibition does not exclude the existence of legal and equitable rights in the same land by more than one person. For example, where one individual has legal title but another contributes to the improvement of the property, equity may recognize a constructive trust placing a beneficial interest in favour of the contributor.[180]

7. The settlement council can force a sale or apply for subdivision of Metis title, provisional Metis title or an allotment if the holder of the interest fails to pay charges, levies, or taxes owed to the settlement in relation to that interest.[181]

8. A settlement may expropriate any interest, less than the fee simple, for the purposes of the settlement if authorized by the *Metis Settlements Land Protection Act* and settlement by-law.[182]

9. The Land Policy does not address the transfer of Metis title from one settlement member to another. Rather, the policy contemplates the acquisition of Metis title through conversion of pre-existing interests, grants from the settlement to holders of provisional Metis title and allotments, and inheritance as a result of a member's death. Procedures and limitations for changes in interest holder as a result of a member's death are discussed in further detail below.

10. The holder of Metis title, provisional Metis title or allotment may only make direct use of timber and other nonrenewable surface resources for the purpose of making improvements to the land. This is subject to the right of the settlement to grant rights of removal for nonrenewable contents of the soil (for example, sand, gravel, clay and timber).

Settlement members cannot sell nonrenewable resources for use off the land. Rights other than the right to make direct use of timber and other nonrenewable resources not reserved by the Crown are retained by the settlement. However, a settlement member can acquire additional rights by some other means established by settlement by-law and General Council Policy. The General Council enacted a Timber Policy in June 1991. The policy addresses timber ownership and granting of timber permits for non-domestic use.[183]

11. The holder of Metis title may not grant a lease, license, easement or right of way for exploration or development of natural resources or implementation of authorized projects and development agreements, unless the grant is authorized by settlement by-law and approved by settlement council. These grants may be for as long as is necessary to make the project viable and are not subject to the ten-year limit discussed above.[184] Authorized projects and development agreements are discussed in further detail below.

### Road Titles

In the letters patent granting fee simple title to settlement lands, the province of Alberta retains the right of management of land for highways, roads, intersections and river crossings for the purposes of improvement, maintenance, designation and regulation. The right of management is limited to areas shown on plans of record filed within one year of the coming into force of the *Metis Settlements Land Protection Act* (1 November 1990) and areas included through subsequent amendments to filed plans which are made with the consent of General Counsel and the Crown.[185]

The Land Policy creates road titles in each road in settlement lands. "Road" is defined as a road allowance, or a road shown on a plan filed with the Registrar of the Metis Land Registry. Only the settlement can be registered as the owner of the road title, but a settlement may grant lesser interests in the road title in accordance with General Council Policy. The Registry Regulation contains special provisions to create an interest register for road titles held by the settlement and the recording of lesser interests against such titles. It also provides a mechanism to record the Crown's right of management on the fee simple register.[186]

### Leases and Lesser Interests

Both the settlement and individual holders of Metis title are authorized to lease land to settlement and nonsettlement members. Leases which, together with rights of renewal, would exceed ten years, must be approved by a settlement by-law stating the general nature of the lease and how long it could last if renewal rights were exercised. As previously mentioned, the ten-year rule does not apply to leases required to develop nonrenewable resources or to implement authorized projects or development agreements.[187] Members cannot lease land to nonmembers without settlement approval.

The Land Policy stipulates terms which will be implied into every nonresidential lease unless the lease clearly excludes these terms in writing. The implied promise of the lessor is to allow the lessee to "use the land [including business or other improvements being leased] without interference as long as the [lessee] pay[s] the rent and live[s] up to the terms of the lease agreement."[188] The implied promises of the lessee are as follows:

(1) I will pay the rent at the times and in the way, the agreement requires;

(2) I will pay any charges, levies or taxes related to the ownership or use of the premises during the lease;

(3) I will take care of the land [including buildings and other improvements] and return it in good condition at the end of the lease;

(4) If the land includes farm land, I will work it according to good farming practice;

(5) If given reasonable notice, I will let you or your representative enter the land to inspect its condition;

(6) If given written notice that I am not living up to the agreement, I will correct the situation within a reasonable time; and if I have not corrected it within 2 months I will let you take the land back without interference.[189]

Many of the implied terms in this section are modified versions of standard terms contained in commercial agreements which have been litigated before, and interpreted by, the courts. Legalese is avoided in the Land Policy to help avoid interpretive problems. For example, the lessor's promise is analogous to the common law covenant of quiet enjoyment subject to the payment of rent and compliance with conditions in the lease agreement. The lessor has a right of forfeiture and re-entry upon the breach of the lessee's promises. The latter covenant has historically been construed strictly against the landlord. Areas of uncertainty are traditionally resolved in favour of the lessee.[190]

As previously noted, holders of Metis title may also transfer lesser interests including licenses, easements, and utility rights of way subject to certain conditions on length and the purpose for transferring the interest. The title of individual holders of Metis title is also subject to certain rights of access and removal authorized by settlement council by-laws and General Council Policy on resource development. Any benefit, including money paid or other consideration given for such grants, belong to the settlement. All Metis title holders can grant leases, licenses, easement or other rights of way to explore and develop nonrenewable resources and to implement authorized projects and development agreements if the grant is permitted by a settlement by-law which approves the specific grant.[191]

## PREVAILING RIGHTS AND INTERESTS

Rights and interests contained in the Land Policy, Registry Regulation and other provincial enactments may operate to limit the rights and interests of the General Council, settlements and settlement members. It is beyond the scope of this book to review all potential conflicts with provincial legislation and consequential amendments or regulations required to address these concerns. Rather, comments on other provincial enactments are limited to the *Water Resources Act, Dower Act, Matrimonial Property Act, Limitation of Actions Act* and *Landlord and Tenant Act.*

### Land Policy

Section 2.4 identifies prevailing interest which overrides the interests of the holder of Metis title. This section provides Metis title is subject to "natural rights of light, air, water and support" and "traditional community pathways and uses."[192]

Natural rights are rights of landowners protected by the common law of torts. The most important and clearly recognized is the right to support; that is, the right of a landowner to have his or her land supported by that of a neighbour. Natural rights to water include the right to obstruct or interfere with the flow of underground water and the rights of riparian owners (that is, a person who owns property abutting upon a body of water) to riparian water.[193] The rights of riparian owners to diversion and use of water are restricted by the *Water Resources Act*. The restrictions arising from the application of this Act are discussed in further detail below.

As rights to light are traditionally associated with buildings and natural rights do not arise in respect of buildings, the right to light is not a natural right of property. Rather, a right to light is an easement acquired by express grant or prescription.[194] The easement of light is the right which the owner of a dominant tenement may acquire to prevent the owner or occupier of an adjoining tenement from building or placing on the land anything which has the effect of obstructing light. Section 50 of the *Limitation of Actions Act* provides that easements to light can no longer be acquired by prescription. It reads as follows:

No right to the use and access of light or any other easement, right in

46

gross or profit *à prendre* shall be acquired by a person by prescription, and it shall be deemed that no such right has ever been acquired.[195]

Although the General Council has the power to create unique interests in land, it is not expressly granted the power to exclude the application of the *Limitation of Actions Act*. Therefore, it is questionable whether a right to light is an enforceable right regardless of the intentions of General Council in absence of consequential amendments to the *Limitation of Actions Act*, or a regulation passed by the Minister to resolve questions or difficulties arising from the application of the Act.

The reference to a natural right to air is ambiguous. The right to the passage of air over one's neighbour's land is similar to an easement for light. Again, the ability to acquire this right by prescription has been abolished by s.50 of the *Limitation of Actions Act*. On the other hand, the right to freedom from smell and noise is a natural right that may be protected by the law of nuisance. Further, the common law recognizes that the owner of the land is also owner of the airspace above his or her land. However, case law suggests this right is restricted by the balancing of the owner's ordinary and potential use and enjoyment of the land against the rights of the general public to take advantage of what science now offers in the use of airspace. This will influence the extent of the owner's rights in actions for interference with airspace by transient invasions (for example, airplanes) and permanent invasions (for example, telephone wires).[196]

The reference to "traditional community pathways and uses" is included to protect local customary rights exercisable by members of the settlements. Examples given in the Land Policy include regular use of pathways and certain parcels as berry-picking areas for many years.[197] Local customary rights are recognized by the common law of property if they are ancient, certain, reasonable and continuous. Again the prohibition against the acquisition of rights of use by prescription in s.50 of the *Limitation of Actions Act* must be considered in assessing the validity of this provision. It is beyond the scope of this book to discuss the existence of Metis aboriginal rights. It should be noted that the absence of clear and plain language abrogating aboriginal rights in s.50, and the potential operation of the settlements legislation as an affirmation or extinguishment of aboriginal rights, may also affect the assessment of the right of the General Council to protect these interests.

### Registry Regulation

A person who records or registers an interest in the Metis Registry can rely on his or her interest being enforced with priority based on the time of its recording in accordance with the date it is recorded. In theory, once recorded or registered, interests are subject only to prior interest which are recorded or registered and pre-existing interests which comply with the conditions for enforcement discussed earlier in this book. However, in practice almost all registry systems, including the Metis Registry system, recognize the priority of certain interests which override the registration system of conferring priorities.

The Metis Settlements Land Registry Regulation provides that the following interests will override the Metis register:

(a) an interest of the Crown in the right of Alberta reserved in, excepted from or set out as a condition to the fee simple granted to the General Council under letters patent;

(b) a lien in favour of a settlement against an interest of a taxpayer for the amount of unpaid taxes, fees, assessments, rates or other charges;

(c) a leasehold for a term of three years or less if:

   (i) there is actual possession of the land under the lease, and
   (ii) that possession could be discovered through reasonable investigation;

(d) an interest created under an enactment that expressly refers to this Regulation and expressly provides that the interest is enforceable with priority other than as provided in this Regulation.[198]

The interests listed are modelled on those recognized as deserving special protection in the proposals for the *Model Land Recording and Registration Act*.[199] The first interest is included in recognition of the public interest in retaining reservations from title, such as mines and minerals, and the collective interests of the settlement members to enforce conditions on title stipulated for their benefit. An example of the latter is the prohibition on alienation without obtaining the requisite consent of the Crown, General Council, and settlement members. The priority given to tax liens recognizes that it is "not practicable to keep up to date tax information in the land registration office," the practice of settlement taxation will be known to a person acquiring interests in settlement lands, and that those who acquire interests "will not fall into the trap of thinking that because the [settlements'] claim is not shown on the land register it does not exist."[200] The recognition of short-term leases assumes that "requiring short term leases to be recorded or registered would be an unconscionable burden on tenants and upon land registration offices."[201]

## Provincial Legislation

*Water Resources Act*

The provincial Crown retains property in water within the boundaries of settlement lands and the right of diversion and use of all water on settlement lands. This reflects the intent of the Crown to limit rights to water which may be recognized in law. However, the extent of the limitation is not clear. Metis people likely are intended to have the same rights to water as other citizens of the province. Water rights are regulated by the *Water Resources Act*. The Act limits the rights of riparian owners (people who own land abutting upon bodies of water) to use and flow. However, the extent to which this legislation has abolished all riparian water rights is uncertain.[202] As there is nothing in the settlements legislation to suggest that the Act does not apply, these same limitations and uncertainties may arise in the interpretation of the rights of Metis riparian owners.

Briefly, riparian rights are restricted to riparian owners. At common law, riparian owners are entitled to receive the flow of water to their property undiminished in quantity *and quality*, subject to the rights of other riparian owners to use the water for domestic purposes. Water can be used for nondomestic purposes so long as the use does not diminish perceptibly the flow to downstream riparian owners. The *Water Resources Act* is concerned with rights of flow, but it does not explicitly address the issue of quality giving rise to the argument that riparian rights associated with the quality of water continue to exist at common law.[203]

The Act sets up a system of licensing for the diversion and use of water, but preserves the common law rights of riparian owners to use water for domestic purposes without obtaining a license or permit. The Act incorporates by reference the definition of land in s.1(n) of the *Land Titles Act* which is broad enough to include settlement land and arguably any unique interests in that land created by General Council Policy. The common law right to domestic use is narrowed through a legislated definition of domestic purposes.[204] It is debatable whether a corollary of the preservation of the right to domestic use is that riparian owners are able to bring actions to restrain licensed or unlicensed diversions of water that impair their use of water for domestic purposes.[205] The *Water Resources Act* is currently being revised. Given the above analysis, future amendments to the Act may also affect the riparian rights of the General Council.

*Law of Property Act* and *Dower Act*

Sections 3 and 4 of the *Law of Property Act* abolish common law dower rights in land and the rights of husbands to estates by curtesy in lands of his deceased wife.[206] At common law, both dower and curtesy arose on the death of the husband or wife respectively. At common law, land descended to an heir related by blood to the landowner. The common law dower evolved to protect limited rights of a surviving female spouse in the property of her deceased husband. Dower entitled the widow to one-third of her husband's freehold property.[207] Under common law a man acquired the right to use and manage the freehold property of his wife for the duration of the marriage or until the birth of children. When the children were born, the husband's interest changed to curtesy. Through

49

curtesy, the husband was entitled to a life estate in all of the real property held by his wife.

Rights of a spouse to interests in land held by a deceased spouse are now governed by the *Dower Act*. Originally the legislation only granted dower rights to widows. However, subsequent amendments to the legislation have extended dower rights to widowers. Given the broad language used in the *Law of Property Act*, the priority of provincial law over General Council Policies, and the failure of the *MSA* to expressly exclude the application of the *Law of Property Act* and the *Dower Act*, one could argue that common law rights of the Metis to dower and curtesy are abolished and the *Dower Act* applies.[208] The application of the *Dower Act* is presumed in the Land Policy and the Registry Regulation. The Land Policy provides that rules governing the descent of property do not affect "rights provided by the *Dower Act* or settlement by-law that would enable a deceased's spouse to continue living on the homestead when the Metis title holder dies."[209] The Registry Regulation addresses the right to prevent disposition without consent, a right which is also recognized under the *Dower Act*.

Homestead is defined in the Land Policy as "the parcel of land where the house in which the Metis title holder lives is located."[210] It is clear from this definition that the dower right to a life estate is not intended to apply to lesser interests such as provisional Metis title and allotments. These interests are most similar to leasehold interests created at common law. It is debatable whether the life estate under the *Dower Act* is intended to apply to leasehold interests. As indicated, the law of dower evolved in relation to freehold estates. Further, as the *Dower Act* grants a life estate to widows and widowers, it would not make sense to give them a greater interest in land than that held by a leaseholder. The alternative argument is that the rights under the *Dower Act* would necessarily be limited to the rights of the survivor to the reversionary interest.

The Land Policy also provides that the life estate in the homestead can be acquired by a spouse who is not a settlement member, but that the estate held by a nonsettlement member cannot be transferred without the consent of the settlement council.[211] The latter limitation is important as the common law recognizes the right of life tenants to alienate a life estate. The common law also imposes certain duties on a life tenant such as duty to pay taxes and liability for waste. The intent of the limitation in the Land Policy may be the reconciliation of the life estate with rights attributed to nonmember spouses under the *MSA*.[212] The *MSA* addresses the rights of nonsettlement family members to reside on settlement lands. Rights of residency are not defined at common law, in the Land Policy or in the

*MSA*. The simple meaning of "reside" is to live, dwell, stay or remain on land and it normally will not include a right of alienation.[213]

The *Dower Act* does not contain a definition of spouse, but it is clear that the Act is only intended to apply to married persons. However, the Land Policy includes someone who has "lived with the deceased as husband or wife and was treated as such by the community" in the definition of deceased's spouse.[214] If the intent is to recognize the right of common law spouses to life estates, this cannot be accomplished by recognizing their rights under the *Dower Act* because they do not have them. Rights of these persons may depend on whether they are settlement or nonsettlement members, the settlement by-laws and the application of equitable doctrines, such as the doctrine of constructive trust discussed earlier in this book.

The Land Policy only addresses rights of surviving spouses to the homestead. However, the *Dower Act* recognizes other dower rights. For example, the surviving spouse, also has a life estate in some of the personal property of the deceased spouse.[215] The *Dower Act* also grants rights that enable a spouse to protect his or her life estate. These rights include the right to prevent disposition of the homestead by withholding consent, the right of an action for damages for disposition without consent where the disposition results in the registration of title in the name of another person, and the right to obtain payment from the Land Titles Assurance Fund where judgement against a spouse who makes a disposition without consent is unsatisfied.[216] The definition of a disposition is broad enough to include agreements for sale, leases for more than three years, mortgages, encumbrances and a devise or disposition made by will.[217] Given the extent of the rights granted under the *Dower Act*, it remains unclear which rights are appropriately applied to settlement lands. Arguably, all of these rights could apply to Metis title given its similarity to a freehold interest at common law, the anticipation of the application of the *Dower Act* in the Land Policy and provisions in the Registry Regulation which contemplate the application of the right to prevent disposition without consent. The Registry Regulation requires the filing of an affidavit of marital status where dower consent for the disposition of Metis title, provisional Metis title, allotments and leases is not obtained.[218] Despite the attempt to apply the *Dower Act* to settlement lands, there are several difficulties in the application of the legislation. Only "homesteads" as defined by the Act are subject to dower rights. The Act is silent on the nature of the legal interest the owner of a homestead must have but the history of the legislation suggests it is intended to apply to fee simple interests. As the interests created by the settlements scheme are unique, arguably they are not contemplated by the legislation. Further, the *Dower Act* assumes the application of the provincial *Land Titles Act*. The *Land Titles Act* does not apply to settlement lands unless specifically incorporated.[219]

Although it may be desirable for certain provisions of the *Law of Property Act* to apply to settlement lands, such as the provisions abolishing dower and tenancy by curtesy, many sections of this Act assume a system of landholding that is inapplicable to the settlement lands. It is beyond the scope of this book to detail the provisions which should or should not be applied to the settlement Metis. However, it should be noted that many provisions assume rights of co-ownership and the ability to devise interests in land under the *Wills Act*. The Land Policy prohibits co-ownership interests in Metis title, allotments and provisional Metis title. Section s.7.5(2) of the Land Policy stipulates that the *Wills Act* does not apply to interests in patented land. Further, provisions in the *Law of Property Act* concerning the enforcement of mortgages and agreements for sale could result in orders granting legal title or orders for sale of the property. Although General Council may develop a policy which allows interests in less than the fee simple to be given as security, they would likely want to develop unique procedures and remedies that protect the rights of secured parties but avoid the possible granting of interests in land to nonmembers. These inconsistencies suggest that the Act may not apply despite the absence of an express exclusion in the *MSA*. Again, a ministerial regulation or amendments to the *Law of Property Act* may be necessary to resolve inconsistencies.

*Matrimonial Property Act*

Section 3 of the *Matrimonial Property Act* states conditions that must be met before a spouse has the right to apply to court for a matrimonial property order.[220] These conditions are broad enough to give rise to rights to apply for division of matrimonial property by members of the Metis settlements. The Act also assumes the application of the *Land Titles Act* and the ability to devise interests by will. Procedures and rights under the Act could result in property rights in land being granted to a nonsettlement spouse. Consequently, some consideration must be given to the appropriateness of applying the *Matrimonial Property Act* to divisions of Metis property, in particular, interests in settlement lands. Again, it is beyond the scope of this book to recommend amendments to provincial legislation; however, it is clear that some thought should be given to potential conflicts and the desirability and constitutionality of delegating the division of interests in settlement lands to the Appeal Tribunal. In the case of Metis lands, it may be more appropriate to limit rights of nonsettlement members to payment of compensation and perhaps some form of residency right. The extent to which a court will be bound by the requirement that Metis title only be held by settlement members is uncertain. However, it is unlikely that a court would grant a matrimonial property order clearly contrary to the legislation and the scheme of landholding envisioned.

*Limitation of Actions Act*: Adverse Possession

People who acquire interests in land by entering the land and staying on it are called adverse possessors and the process by which they acquire title is called adverse possession. The theory of adverse possession is based on limitation periods. Where a landowner fails to take legal steps to get rid of an adverse possessor within a reasonable time, the landowner loses the right of recovery and the adverse possessor gains rights to the land.

Statutes of limitation now govern the law of adverse possession. In Alberta, s.18 of the *Limitation of Actions Act* places a ten-year limitation period on proceedings to recover land.[221] The definition of land includes freehold and leasehold estates and is arguably broad enough to include the unique interests created under the settlements system. Failure to take action to recover land within the limitation period may result in the extinguishment of the landowner's rights to land and recognition of adverse possession by a squatter who has possession in law. Whether a squatter has sufficient possession in law varies with the facts of each case. Upon receiving a favourable judgement from the court, s.74 of the *Land Titles Act* allows the adverse possessor to file his or her judgement at the Land Titles Office.[222] It also gives the Registrar the power to revise title and issue a new certificate of title accordingly.

Section 99 of the *MSA* states that rights or interests in settlement lands may exist "under a provision of this *or another Act*" (emphasis added).[223] Consequently, a right of adverse possession by settlement members may arise by operation of the *Limitation of Actions Act*. On the other hand, the *Limitation of Actions Act* anticipates the application of the *Land Titles Act* which does not apply, unless expressly incorporated, to settlement lands. Further, a provision similar to s.74 of the *Land Titles Act* does not appear in the Registry Regulation. Finally, the Land Policy envisions all entitlements being subject to settlement approval. This suggests title can not be acquired by adverse possession. However, consequential amendments or a ministerial regulation may be required to clarify this position.

*Landlord and Tenant Act*

The settlement legislation does not expressly exclude the application of the *Landlord and Tenant Act*. It is unlikely that the General Council has the power to exclude its application for the reasons given in preliminary comments to this section. As provisional Metis title creates a tenancy and is most similar to a leasehold at common law, the *Landlord and Tenant Act* may apply to this interest in limited circumstances. The effect of the legislation will vary depending upon whether the tenancy created is residential or nonresidential. A residential tenancy agreement is defined in the *Landlord and Tenant Act* as a "written, oral or implied agreement to rent residential premises."[224] One might argue that the reference to "rent" requires the payment of consideration. Therefore, provisional Metis title will never create a residential tenancy. However, the term "to rent" may refer to the creation of a tenancy, rather than the payment of consideration. Assuming this argument is accepted, there is still some difficulty bringing provisional Metis title within the definition of a residential tenancy agreement because the chances of the agreement granting exclusive possession to residential premises are very remote. Land is the subject of provisional Metis title. Homes are to be built by the recipient of title, rather than the settlement. The home is an improvement which may be removed by the tenant when the term of provisional title expires and Metis title is not subsequently granted. However, the home may become the property of the settlement on failure of the member to remove it within a specified time. In the event the land and home are subsequently granted by the settlement to another member by way of provisional Metis title, a residential tenancy agreement may be created.

The *Landlord and Tenant Act* states that "any waiver or release by a tenant of residential premises of the rights, benefits or protections provided to him under the Act is void."[225] Given this, provisions in the Memorandum of Provisional Metis Title that are inconsistent with the legislation could be of no effect if the tenancy created is residential. Even though the chance of creating a residential tenancy is remote, the Memorandum should be reviewed for the purpose of identifying inconsistencies. Any other settlement by-laws or regulations passed under s.2.3(3) of the Land Policy should be subjected to the same scrutiny.

If the *Landlord and Tenant Act* is applied, the tenancy-like relationships created by provisional Metis title will more likely be affected by provisions which apply to tenancies "other than residential tenancies." Conflicting provisions are not an issue because the Act allows contracting out.[226] However, provisions in the Act which apply to nonresidential tenancies might be implied if not expressly excluded. Section 99 of the *Land Titles Act* also contains implied covenants.[227] However, s.104(2) of the *MSA* states that the *Land Titles Act* will not apply with respect to patented land in the settlement areas unless otherwise provided by the Registry Regulation. As the Regulation does not incorporate s.99 of the *Land Titles Act*, these terms will not be implied into nonresidential tenancies.

As the Memorandum of Allotment prohibits the construction of a "permanent house" on the land, the chances of creating a residential tenancy are even more remote.[228] Nevertheless, comments relating to the application of provisions in the *Landlord and Tenant Act* to nonresidential tenancies apply.

## Descent of Property

The Land Policy establishes special rules governing the devolution of interests in land upon the death of the settlement member. The extent to which this process affects the characterization of interests in land has been discussed above and will not be repeated here. Comments in this section are limited to a discussion of the estate instructions system, and the application of the *Intestate Succession Act* and the *Ultimate Heir Act*.

Estate Instructions

General Council has excluded the application of the *Wills Act* to interests in patented lands.[229] Instead, the Land Policy creates a unique system whereby interests in land are transferred on death by way of estate instructions.[230] Estate instructions are written instructions filed at the Metis Land Registry saying "what should be done with a members interest in land when he or she dies."[231] The Land Policy prohibits the transfer of part, but not all, of the deceased's interests in the land by estate instruction. This prohibition prevents a physical division in the transfer of property, and likely the creation of successive future interests in the land. Arguably, it is broad enough to prevent any kind of a conditional transfer which could be interpreted as transferring only part of the estate because of future rights retained by the deceased or persons designated by the deceased.[232]

Estate instructions are to be in the form attached to the Land Policy (Appendix 5, Part 7). Instructions may include an heirs list, may name a land trustee to hold the land for the purpose of dealing with the land in accordance with estate instructions, provide for what is to be done with the interest if no one on the heirs list takes it, and give directions to sell the interest and have the money distributed as part of the deceased's personal estate.[233] The heirs list is "a list of persons named in the estate instructions in order of priority for consideration to receive interests in land when the holder dies."[234] If a land trustee is not appointed, the settlement becomes the land trustee unless the settlement council appoints someone else. The land trustee holds the deceased's estate only for the purpose of dealing with the land according to the estate instructions, settlement by-laws and the Land Policy. The trustee is to administer the instructions to the extent possible to give effect to the wishes of the deceased. A trustee who fails to carry out his or her duties can be replaced by the settlement council.[235] Changes in the instructions may be filed with the Registrar during the holder's lifetime.[236]

55

*Intestate Succession Act*

Sections 7.12 and 7.13 of the Land Policy address the distribution of property where there are no estate instructions.[237] These provisions may cause some concern as there is no explicit power in the *MSA* for the General Council to exclude the application of the *Intestate Succession Act*. However, General Council is given the general power to create policy relating to the devolution of interests whether the member dies testate or intestate. Although the term intestate presumes the ability to devise property by way of will, this term is not defined in the *Intestate Succession Act*. Given the common understanding of the term, the powers of the General Council to make policy, and the exclusion of the *Wills Act*, one might argue this is sufficient to render the *Intestate Succession Act* inapplicable to interests held in Metis lands.

Perhaps a more significant concern is the process enabling the trustee to apply to the settlement council, and subsequently the Appeal Tribunal, for direction if there are no estate instructions, instructions are uncertain, or the interest has not been transferred within twenty-one years of the anniversary of the deceased's death.[238] These functions are traditionally exercised by the Court of Queen's Bench. Therefore, there may be an issue relating to the constitutionality of the process envisioned. Section 7.13 outlines the guiding principles to be considered when application is made by the trustee. These are:

(a) as far as possible, and to the extent that they can be clearly determined, the last wishes of the deceased should be met;

(b) the interest must be transferred to the deceased's spouse if it can be registered in his or her name, and if there is more land than can be registered in the spouse's name, the spouse can specify the order in which the interests should be considered for registration;

(c) if there are one or more living adults on the heirs list and they agree on what should be done with the interest, the agreement should be followed;

(d) if it is not possible to get an agreement from the persons on the heirs list but, in the opinion of the body making the decision, there is substantial agreement among adult members of the deceased's family as to what should be done with the interest, that agreement should be followed;

(e) if there are no adult members of the deceased's family, but the deceased leaves living children, the land interest should be given to the child who, in the opinion of the settlement council, is best able to use it for the purpose intended;

(f) if it is not possible within a reasonable time to decide who should receive the interest in accordance with the above principles, the land should be sold and the money made part of the deceased's estate.

7.13(2) In this section "deceased's family" means the adult members of the deceased's immediate family, if there are any, and otherwise the adult members of the deceased's extended family.

Finally, some consideration should be given to the application of the *Ultimate Heir Act*. Under this legislation, if a person dies intestate and there is no one to take the land in accordance with the distribution scheme under the *Intestate Succession Act*, title reverts to the Crown. On settlement lands the land is to be sold and made part of the deceased's personal estate if there is no one to take it under the scheme envisioned by section 7.13. This and the reference to "dying intestate" in the *Ultimate Heir Act* suggest it is inapplicable to settlement lands.

# Land Use Planning   6

Land use planning is used here to refer to the system of regulation of land use and development envisioned by the Metis settlements legislation. Elsewhere in Alberta, the system of land use planning is established under the *Alberta Planning Act* and related statutes.[239] The *MSA* provides that the *Planning Act* is amended so that it does not apply to the geographic area of the Metis settlements.[240] Also, as soon as is reasonably possible, the Minister of Municipal Affairs must amend the boundaries of those improvement districts in which settlement areas are located so that the settlements cease to be a part of those areas.[241] However, as the system of planning is modelled after the provincial system, it is useful to briefly review the provincial system before examining the system adopted on settlement lands.

Under the *Planning Act*, development essentially comprises three components:

(a) the division of a unit of land into smaller units to accommodate their disposition;

(b) the construction of structures on a unit of land; and

(c) the use to which the land is put.[242]

The Act itself does not regulate how land is to be used. Rather, it delegates tasks necessary for effective planning and regulation to a number of authorities created under it or other provincial legislation. These authorities are referred to as planning agencies. The *Planning Act* also provides for a hierarchy of planning instruments, regulations and by-laws through which planning and development are controlled.

Planning agencies are established at the provincial, regional and municipal level. The most important planning agencies are discussed briefly below:

1. The Lieutenant Governor in Council is responsible for creating planning regions and appointing members of the Alberta Planning Board. In addition, this agency has numerous other responsibilities including establishing subdivision standards, regulating potential dangerous uses of land, and regulating the equivalent of land use

by-laws which are to be in force until a municipality enacts its own by-laws.

2. The Minister of Municipal Affairs is responsible for planning in the province. In particular he or she administers the planning fund, serves as a subdivision authority in improvement districts not covered by a planning area (or alternatively authorizes a municipality to serve this function), and prepares and adopts regional plans.

3. The Alberta Planning Board has five main functions: reviewing and making recommendations to the Minister relating to the ratification of regional plans, hearing appeals from the regional planning commission, resolving intermunicipal disputes, hearing appeals from subdivision authorities, and advising the Minister and province in planning matters.

4. Regional Planning Commissions are composed of members from various local governments falling within planning regions created by the Lieutenant Governor in Council. Currently there are ten planning regions in Alberta. The main function of the Regional Planning Commission is to prepare and adopt regional plans for the area and to serve as a subdivision-approving authority. It also provides advice and assistance to member municipalities.

5. Municipal councils may establish Municipal Planning Commissions and appoint members to Regional Planning Commissions where appropriate. In addition, if the population of the municipality is over 1,000, a Development Appeal Board may be established. In municipalities where the population is less than 1,000, the council serves as the Development Appeal Board.

6. The Municipal Planning Commission receives, processes and decides whether or not to issue development permit applications. In some municipalities, this task is divided between the Commission and development officers. In some instances the Commission may be authorized to act as a subdivision authority (for example, Calgary and Edmonton).

7. Development officers receive applications for development permits. These people are usually salaried employees of the municipality. Development officers also have the power to issue stop-work orders stopping unauthorized use or development.

8. Development Appeal Boards hear appeals of persons affected by decisions of Municipal Planning Commissions and Development Officers.[243]

Rules and regulations for the development of land are established through a hierarchy of planning instruments. The general rule is that a

development will not be approved if it is not in accordance with a planning by-law which in turn must be consistent with development plans and regulations. At the top of the hierarchy are provincial regulations that relate to dangerous use, airport vicinity, special planning areas and subdivision. Regional and local plans must conform with these regulations. The main thrust of the Subdivision Regulation is to prescribe procedures for obtaining subdivision approval and standards for the location of certain kinds of subdivisions such as highways and sewage plants. Next in the hierarchy are regional plans consisting of maps and statements setting down the pattern of land use and development for the area and outlining the goals and objectives of the planning regions covered. These are followed by municipal plans (which apply to the geographic area of the municipality), area structure plans (which apply to a finite area of the municipality), area redevelopment plans, land use by-laws and the approval processes established for subdivisions and development permits. Land use by-laws prescribe the system of permits for a municipality and the procedural and substantive rules to be followed by a decision maker dealing with applications. They also prescribe, in considerable detail, the uses and developments which may or may not be effected in each unit of land located in a municipality. More specifically, they establish land use categories that apply to finite areas in the municipality and development standards that must be met in the process of development.[244]

## SETTLEMENT LAND USE PLANNING

### Planning Administration Under the Settlements Legislation

The *MSA* also creates a number of planning agencies and instruments similar to those found in the provincial land use planning regime. Like the provincial *Planning Act*, the *MSA* does not purport to plan and regulate how land is to be used. Rather, these powers are delegated to planning agencies. Planning for all settlement areas is controlled by the Lieutenant Governor in Council, the Minister, the Commissioner of the Metis Settlements Transition Commission and the General Council. Local settlement land use and development is controlled by General Council and settlement councils. General Council and settlement councils do not have a role in planning outside of the settlement areas. This could be of some concern for Peavine and Gift Lake which have been pulled out of the South Peace regional planning area, but which may still be affected indirectly by the regional planning for the area.[245] Consequently, the exemption of the settlements from provincial planning legislation requires that further attention be paid to the creation of agencies or processes that enable an effective interface between settlements and adjacent jurisdictions.

The most important planning agencies in the settlements and their principle functions are as follows:

1. The Lieutenant Governor in Council may make regulations of general or specific application prohibiting and regulating the development or use of land in the vicinity of airports, prohibiting and regulating development that may create a danger to the health or welfare of persons or property, authorizing a member of the executive council or settlement councils to exercise powers or duties under the regulations and directing settlement councils to amend by-laws to conform with development regulations.[246]

2. The Minister is also responsible for making subdivision regulations.[247] The Minister also receives and approves General Council Policies, including those related to land use and development. A portion of a policy or a policy that is vetoed has no effect. The Minister may specify that such policies are not subject to approval by regulation at the request of the General Council.[248]

For the first three years following the enactment of the MSA, all settlement by-laws must also be prepared in consultation with, and approved by, the Minister unless the Minister passes a regulation specifying the subject matter of by-laws for which consultation and approval is not necessary. The Minister may also make by-laws by way of regulation within the first three years in areas that are within the jurisdiction of settlement councils. These may be appealed or amended by the settlements.[249]

3. General Council may, after consultation with the Minister, enact policies "providing for planning, land use and development of settlement areas, including the prohibition or regulation and control of the use and development of lands and buildings."[250] The existing Land Policy establishes some rules controlling the process of application for member interests in settlement lands and the size, use and development of Metis title, provisional Metis title and allotments.[251] The Land Policy contemplates that more detailed conditions and planning for use and development will be addressed in settlement land management by-laws that conform with general Land Policy.

4. Under the regulations, the subdivision-approving authority for all of the settlements is the Commissioner.[252] As the Commissioner is intended to have transitional authority only, this function should eventually be delegated to either the General Council, the settlements or some other agency approved by ministerial regulation.

5. The most important function of the settlement council in the area of

planning is the development of settlement plans and land use by-laws. Settlement councils may make by-laws:

   (a) establishing a general plan for land use and development in the settlement area;
   (b) prohibiting or regulating and controlling the use and development of land and buildings in the settlement area;
   (c) authorizing the settlement council, or a person designated by it, to prohibit the development or use of land or buildings if there are inadequate arrangements for access to, and for utilities and other services to, the land or buildings.[253]

The *MSA* also provides for powers of inspection and by-law enforcement by officers appointed by the settlement and approved by the Minister. Alternatively, agreements may be entered with the Minister on behalf of an improvement district, a municipal authority or other local authority for joint law enforcement. Persons served with enforcement notices have recourse to the Appeal Tribunal.[254]

The settlement has the authority to develop a system for granting permits, approvals and licenses and prohibiting development until a permit is obtained.[255] The settlement council may function as an approving authority in receiving, processing and deciding upon permit applications or this power may be delegated to one or more persons. However, permits, leases, licenses and other authorizations issued under the former *Metis Betterment Act* continue with the same effect as if they had been issued by settlement council.[256] The jurisdiction of the settlement will necessarily be limited by General Council Policy. However, additional conditions on use and development may be placed by settlement by-law.

The settlement may also make by-laws in other areas affecting land use. These include: (i) the regulation of activities and equipment in parks, recreational areas, trailer courts, mobile home parks, campgrounds, exhibition grounds and rodeo grounds; (ii) regulation and control of use of water sources and compelling the removal of obstructions which endanger the public health of settlement members; (iii) control and regulation of business in the settlement area; (iv) installation of water and sewage connections; and (v) subject to an act of Parliament, controlling, operating and maintaining an airport, aerodrome or seaplane base.[257] The settlement also has direction, control and management of highways and roads within the settlement area not subject to the exercise of the rights by the province.[258]

6. The Appeal Tribunal has jurisdiction to hear appeals in land use planning matters. In particular, it has authority to hear appeals from decisions of the General Council or settlement councils in matters

relating to the granting of interests in settlement land as stipulated in the Land Policy.[259] It also has authority to hear appeals from decisions of the subdivision-approving authority.[260] The *MSA* also provides that the Appeal Tribunal has jurisdiction to hear any appeals and references (or to perform other functions) required under regulation, by-laws or General Council Policies. It may also hear other disputes if the parties to the dispute agree.[261] Consequently, the jurisdiction of the Appeal Tribunal may be expanded in land use matters as disputes arise or specific land-use policies and by-laws are developed. Appeals on questions of law or jurisdiction lie to the Court of Appeal after leave to appeal has been obtained.[262]

7. In addition to acting as the subdivision-approving authority, the Commissioner may play an advisory and assistance role in the administration and development of the powers of, and programs and procedures developed by, the General Council and settlement councils. The Commissioner may also help to coordinate policies, programs and procedures with those of the Crown.[263]

### Planning Instruments

The planning scheme for the settlement area also creates a hierarchy of planning instruments which will reflect the goals and objectives of settlement planning. These instruments include the *MSA*, regulations, General Council Policy, settlement plans, and settlement by-laws. The general rule is: development will not be approved if it does not conform to settlement by-laws, which in turn must be consistent with settlement plans, General Council Policy, regulations, the *MSA* and other provincial planning legislation (such as the *Public Health Act* and the *Public Highways Development Act*), most of which are applicable to Metis settlements.

Most of the relevant provisions in the *MSA* relating to planning have been discussed. In addition, there are special provisions relating to the subdivision of land.[264] Although development on the settlements is subject to hazardous use regulations, a special regulation has yet to be enacted relating to provincial or settlement lands. Dangerous uses are addressed in the context of standards and locations of specific kinds of subdivisions in the Alberta Subdivision Regulations (for example, location of subdivisions in relation to landfill sites and sewage treatment plants), but these provisions do not apply to the settlements which have their own subdivision regulation.[265] The issue of dangerous use in this context is left to the discretion of the subdivision-approving authority or a decision resulting from an appeal to the Appeal Tribunal.

Although detailed planning is left to the settlements through settlement plans and by-laws, few settlement by-laws have been approved as of the date of this book. Settlement land use planning is still in the development stage.

## Subdivision

The *MSA* provides that the Minister may make subdivision regulations.[266] Pursuant to this authority, the Minister has prepared the Metis Settlements Subdivision Regulation. The Registrar of the Metis Settlements Land Registry must not accept any instrument, or caveat that relates to an instrument, that has the effect of subdividing land in the settlement area unless it is a subdivision permitted by s.105 of the *MSA* or is approved by the Subdivision Regulation. Section 105 provides that subdivision or development approval is not required for a highway, public roadway, well or battery (as defined under the *Oil and Gas Conservation Act*), or a pipeline, installation, or structure incidental to the operation of a pipeline.[267]

The main thrust of the Subdivision Regulation is to define subdivisions for the purpose of the *MSA*, establish a subdivision-approving authority, and prescribe procedures to be followed by persons seeking approval to subdivide a parcel of land. It also provides for the registration of subdivisions under the Land Registry Regulation. Standards as to locations of specific kinds of subdivisions and their uses are left to the discretion of the subdivision-approving authority. They may also arise from conditions placed on approval by the settlement in whose area the subdivision is located.

The common understanding of a subdivision is the process by which a person seeks to divide an area of land into smaller parcels for the purpose of obtaining separate titles for each parcel.[268] The definition of subdivision in the Regulation is broader in scope. It includes any plan of subdivision prepared for the purpose of dividing a parcel and the transfer of Metis title, provisional Metis title, allotments and leaseholds.[269] A subdivision does not occur as a result of the establishment of the first fee simple and Metis title registers, the conversion of an interest under the Land Interests Conversion Regulation, or the transfer of an interest in a parcel that does not exceed three years.[270]

The Subdivision Regulation appoints the Commissioner as the subdivision-approving authority. Only a person who is a holder of Metis title, or someone acting on his or her behalf, is entitled to apply to the Commissioner for subdivision approval. Subdivision applications must describe the parcels to be divided and to be created. Applications must be sent by the Commissioner to the settlement in whose area the parcel is located. The Commissioner may also circulate the application, or notice of it, to any other persons or agencies he or she considers appropriate. The

Commissioner has broad discretion and may conduct a hearing before making a decision. Notice of the decision must be given to the applicant and posted in the office of the settlement. Unless permitted by s.105 of the Act, a subdivision is of no effect until approval is granted.[271]

A subdivision application may be refused for "any reason" the Commissioner considers sufficient.[272] Alternatively, the Commissioner may grant conditional approval if the land is suitable for the intended purpose of the subdivision and the subdivision is consistent with settlement legislation, regulations, General Council Policy and settlement by-laws. Conditional approvals are subject to the submission of a plan of subdivision to the Commissioner within one year of the conditional approval and compliance with conditions placed by the Commissioner or the affected settlement council. Conditions in favour of the settlement may be recorded in the Registry. A final grant of subdivision approval must be granted if a plan of subdivision is submitted on time, conditions are complied with, or the settlement is satisfied the conditions it imposes will be complied with. If plans are not submitted on time, the conditional approval is void.[273]

If subdivision approval is granted, the person designated by the Commissioner must sign the plan of subdivision or other document affecting the subdivision, to indicate that approval has been granted.[274] Upon filing of the plan of subdivision in the Metis Land Registry deposit file, the Registrar can cancel relevant registers for the land at issue and create one or more new registers. Notification must be given to the registered owner and all other persons having registered or recorded interests in the register affected. The Registrar may also file plans of survey and descriptive plans prepared under the Registry Regulation or the Subdivision Regulation if requirements set out in the Registry Regulation relating to form, content, authentication and notice to affected settlements are met. The Registrar may require written explanation of discrepancies between plans, land descriptions, or other matters affecting the plan. The Registrar may also correct plans if satisfied that the correction will not adversely affect anyone or anyone adversely affected consents to the correction.[275]

Any person directly affected by the decision may appeal the decision to the Appeal Tribunal. Disputes concerning compliance with conditions may also be referred to the Appeal Tribunal.[276] The Appeal Tribunal, or a court, may also make an order that amends, corrects or cancels part or all of a plan in the deposit file and may transfer any interest of land shown on the plan on application by the settlement, the person who recorded an interest in land shown on the plan, the person who has prepared the plan of survey or descriptive plan, and the Registrar.[277]

# Resource Management 7

As indicated earlier in this book, General Council's fee simple title to the settlement area does not include ownership of mines and minerals. Prior to the proclamation of the settlements legislation (1 November 1991), the authority to dispose of minerals was exercised by the Minister of Energy and surface access fell under the jurisdiction of the provincial Surface Rights Board. Under the new system, the *Surface Rights Act* no longer applies to Metis lands and jurisdiction formerly in the Surface Rights Board is now exercised by panels of the Appeal Tribunal.[278] Further, the Metis acquire greater control over surface access and the Minister's power to dispose of subsurface resources. The Metis settlements system is quite different from that affecting other private landowners "which presumes that a private surface owner can neither prevent the Crown from disposing of subsurface rights nor prevent a subsurface owner from entering their land to access the minerals to which they have a right."[279] The only right of a private owner is to make a case for "fair consideration and compensation resulting from surface disturbance, before the Surface Rights Board."[280]

Pursuant to the *MSA*, Metis may enter agreements for surface entry. If an agreement cannot be reached, a right of entry order (which may or may not be conditional) may be granted by one of two panels of the Appeal Tribunal. Persons who, under a right of entry order, enter the land contrary to the provisions of the *MSA* commit a trespass and are liable in damages to the surface occupant, the settlement council, persons with registered interests in settlement lands and the General Council, depending on the parties affected.[281] The Crown's right to dispose of minerals remains, but special procedures for dispositions after 1 November 1990 are set out in the Co-Management Agreement appended as Schedule 3 to the *MSA*. The Co-Management Agreement also enables the General Council to negotiate overriding royalties (right reserved to receive a share of the portion of production, or value of the portion of production) and participation options (retention of not more than 25 percent undivided interest of the successful bidder) in mineral development agreements entered between third parties and the Crown.[282]

## ACCESS TO SETTLEMENT LANDS

The *MSA* established the Appeal Tribunal as a quasi-judicial body with jurisdiction to hear various disputes including disputes relating to surface rights. Pursuant to the *MSA*, four panels of the Tribunal have been created which may exercise the same jurisdiction of the Tribunal. These are the Existing Leases Land Access Panel (ELLAP), the Land Access Panel (LAP), the Membership Panel and the Land Panel. The first two panels are created under the *MSA* and deal with matters of surface access formerly within the jurisdiction of the Surface Rights Board. The ELLAP consists of a chairperson appointed by the agreement of the Minister and General Council, two members appointed by General Council, one appointed by industry associations and one appointed by the Minister of Energy. The LAP must have at least three members appointed by the Tribunal, one of whom must be a chair appointed by agreement of the General Council and the Minister.[283]

The ELLAP deals exclusively with companies that held mineral leases prior to 1 November 1991 (existing mineral leaseholders). Although the new system respects pre-existing entry rights of mineral leaseholders, if an existing mineral leaseholder does not have an existing right of entry or additional surface access is required, the existing mineral leaseholder must obtain the consent of the occupants of the surface or a right of entry order from the ELLAP.[284] The Land Policy places limits on the right of the surface holder to give consent and enter into private access agreements by way of lease, license, easement or right of way, if any of these instruments are required to explore or develop nonrenewable resources other than contents of the soil.[285] The grant can only be made if it is of a class permitted by settlement by-law and settlement council approves the grant. The practical effect of the policy is the settlement council is also involved in the consent process.

If a private agreement cannot be reached, the existing mineral leaseholder may apply to the ELLAP for a resolution of the dispute. The ELLAP may direct the parties to engage in negotiations, inquire into matters it deems necessary to make a decision, establish other reasonable means for making a decision (including providing the Panel with their final offers), and grant right of entry orders. If a right of entry order is granted, the Panel may limit the purpose of entry, set expiration dates, make the order exclusive to the applicants and set conditions for entry. Once the order is made, the Panel must notify occupants of parcels affected so that representations can be made on the issue of compensation. The Panel may decide the amount of initial and annual compensation to be paid to those affected.[286] Appeals on questions of law or jurisdiction lie to the

Court of Appeal. The Act also gives directions as to costs arising from an appeal.[287]

Operators are subject to a more stringent requirement than existing leaseholders. They must obtain the consent of the General Council, the settlement council and the occupant of the surface or obtain an entry order from the Land Access Panel.[288] Operators include persons permitted to engage in an authorized project as defined by the *MSA*. Authorized projects include a right to work or develop minerals under the Co-Management Agreement after the coming into force of the settlements legislation, and rights arising from provincial legislation such as the *Pipeline Act* and the *Hydro and Electric Energy Act*.[289] An operator who is unable to obtain the requisite consents may apply to the LAP for a right of entry order. The LAP does not have the same powers as the ELLAP regarding negotiations and inquiries; however, it can place the same limits and conditions on right of entry orders. Procedures relating to notice, compensation, and appeal are the same for both panels.[290]

The LAP has additional jurisdiction to review and amend all right of entry orders and compensation orders, regardless of who made them (including orders by the ELLAP and Alberta Surface Rights Board). It may also amend or cancel right of entry orders issued by the ELLAP or LAP if the right of entry order is not being used or there is "another good reason."[291] However, a decision to amend or terminate cannot be made without an inquiry and hearing if requested by the existing mineral leaseholder or operator. Finally, the LAP also has jurisdiction to review rates of compensation under existing mineral leases, and compensation owed by operators under compensation orders and surface leases.[292] A surface lease is defined as any lease or instrument for which land is held, for which a right of entry order may be obtained and that provides for compensation.[293]

## COMPENSATION

Section 118 of the *MSA* sets out factors that the ELLAP and LAP may consider in determining the amount of money payable by an existing mineral leaseholder or operator. These are:

(a) the value of the parcel of land affected, including
    (i) the cultural value for preserving a traditional Metis way of life,
    (ii) the economic value as an asset, and the productive value;

(b) damage in the existing mineral lease or authorized area, including
    (i) the effect of the lease or project on the present and planned use of the parcel surrounding the area,
    (ii) the special damages to improvements, crops, wildlife, livestock, trap lines and natural vegetation resulting from the lease or project, and

(iii) the amount of the lease or project area that the existing mineral lease holder or operator may damage;

(c) the impact of the lease or project on other areas, including
(i) disturbance to the physical, social and cultural environment,
(ii) location of the lease or project in relation to existing or planned community uses, and
(iii) other specific matters, such as cumulative effect of related projects;

(d) any agreement, in addition to a development agreement, entered into by an existing mineral lease holder or operator and the General Council and the occupant;

(e) any other factors the Panel considers appropriate.[294]

The LAP may, without a hearing, amend any compensation order, regardless of who made it, if there has been a change in the existing mineral leaseholder, operator or occupant. Occupant is defined broadly in this case to include the settlement council, the person in actual possession of the surface, and persons with a recorded right or interest in the affected land. If an existing mineral leaseholder or operator fails to pay compensation owing under a surface lease or order of the ELLAP or LAP, the person entitled to receive compensation may file evidence with the LAP of failure to pay. The LAP may direct the provincial Treasurer to pay the amount owing. Where money is paid by the provincial Treasurer, the debt owing becomes a debt owing to the Crown in the right of Alberta.[295]

Compensation payable by existing mineral leaseholders and operators obliged to pay compensation under a surface lease or compensation orders (collectively referred to as obliged operators) may also be reviewed by the LAP. Every four years from the date of the anniversary of the surface lease or right of entry order, obliged operators must advise those entitled to receive payment that they intend to have the rate reviewed if they so desire and that the person receiving notice has the right to have the rate of compensation reviewed or fixed. Upon receiving notice, the parties are obliged to negotiate in good faith for a period of twelve months. If an agreement cannot be reached, either party may apply to the LAP for a hearing and a determination of the rate of compensation. If an obliged operator fails to give the required notice, the party entitled to payment may serve notice on the obliged operator requesting a review of compensation. Again there is an obligation to negotiate in good faith for twelve months before application can be made to the LAP.[296]

The sections dealing with enforcement of payment and review of rates are concerned with compensation orders and surface leases. They do not specifically address development agreements. Development agreements are agreements setting out rights, obligations and conditions attached to a general right to work, explore or develop minerals, including the right of surface access. Parties to the agreement are at least the General Council and settlement council and operators or existing mineral leaseholders. Agreements with operators are governed by the Co-Management Agreement. Disputes relating to rights of entry are within the jurisdiction of the LAP or ELLAP depending on the parties to the agreement. It may be that terms governing disputes relating to compensation provisions in development agreements are to be negotiated by the parties and contained in the agreement itself.[297]

## DISPOSITIONS AFTER 1 NOVEMBER 1991

Metis Settlement Access Committees (MSAC) are established under the terms of the Co-Management Agreement. The MSAC is composed of five members appointed by the Minister of Energy, the Energy Resources Conservation Board, the settlement corporation, the General Council, and the Commissioner. When the position of Commissioner no longer exists, the Commissioner's position is to be filled by a person agreed upon by the other four members. Appointees may sit on more than one MSAC. Upon a recommendation from the Crown Mineral Disposition Review Committee that a public offering for rights in minerals be issued (posting request), the Minister of Energy must, if willing to post the request (that is, issue a notice of public offering), send the posting request to the affected MSAC.[298] Within forty-two days, the MSAC must recommend that the request be denied or that the minerals be posted. The MSAC must also specify any special terms and conditions that are to be included in the document issued by the Minister to solicit bids for the acquisition of rights to minerals (Notice of Public Offering — NPO).[299] Conditions may relate to environmental, sociocultural, and land use impacts and the employment and business opportunities relating to exploration and development of the minerals at issue. Terms and conditions may also address General Council's reservation of an overriding royalty, a participation option, or both.[300]

If the MSAC recommends a posting, then the Minister must prepare an NPO and include those recommended terms and conditions he or she chooses to incorporate. The NPO is then delivered to the MSAC which approves or disapproves of the proposed terms. Unless the Minister decides not to post the minerals, the Minister must resubmit the NPO for approval if the MSAC disapproves of any terms. The procedure is repeated until a satisfactory NPO is drafted or the Minister decides not to post. If the MSAC recommends that the minerals not be posted, the Minister may still grant rights in the minerals but is obliged to advise the recipient that no access will be granted to Metis lands to recover the minerals.[301]

Once the NPO is approved, it is included in the next scheduled public offering of mineral rights. Within two days of the offering, the Minister must provide the General Council and affected settlement with the name of the bidder who has offered the greatest amount of payment and whose bid meets the requirements of the NPO. The General Council and settlement are then able to enter negotiations with the bidder on topics, terms and conditions set out in the NPO which may or may not include overriding royalties and participation options. Within seven days of receiving the name of the bidder, the settlement and General Council must advise the Minister to reject the bid or that they have entered into a development agreement with the bidder. If the bid is rejected, or the Minister does not receive notice within seven days, the Minister must reject the bid and provide the General Council and settlement with the name of the next highest bidder. The process continues until a development agreement can be reached. Occupants who agree to provide access may also be parties to the development agreement. Once an agreement is reached, the Minister has twenty-one days to enter a resource agreement granting the rights in minerals to the successful bidder.[302]

# Hunting, Fishing and Trapping     8

Constitutional jurisdiction over hunting, trapping and fishing is divided between the federal and provincial governments. Alberta has constitutional jurisdiction over game in Alberta which is exercised primarily through the *Wildlife Act*.[303] Special regulations were also passed under the former *Metis Betterment Act* to control "hunting, trapping and killing of game birds, big game or fur bearing animal[s]."[304] The federal government has the jurisdiction to enter into treaties and pursuant to this power has entered into agreements and enacted the *Migratory Birds Convention Act* to establish closed seasons on the hunting of migratory birds.[305] It also has jurisdiction over fisheries, but the practice of the federal government is to make regulations in this area based on advice from the provinces.[306] Under the former legislation, the province enacted regulations limiting hunting, trapping and fishing on settlement lands to settlement members but these rights remained subject to federal legislation on fisheries and migratory birds.[307]

Given the importance of hunting, fishing, trapping and gathering to the traditional Metis economy, special provisions have been included in the *MSA* to address access to, and use of, these resources. As a general rule, by-laws or resolutions that are inconsistent with the *MSA*, or any other provincial enactment, are of no effect to the extent of inconsistency. However, by-laws or resolutions to implement General Council Policy on hunting, trapping, fishing or gathering are given priority over the *MSA* and other provincial law. All by-laws and resolutions must be consistent with General Council Policy.[308] Because of the priority given to General Council Policy in these areas, such policies can only be made in consultation with the Minister. Further they must be approved by all eight settlements and the Lieutenant Governor in Council. In order to protect rare or endangered species, the Lieutenant Governor may rescind any or all aspects of an approval given and repeal part or all of the policy.

The process of approval and powers of General Council and settlements in these areas are set out in the Act:

> 226(1) The General Council may, after consultation with the Minister, make, amend or repeal a Policy in respect of all or any of the matters described in subsection (2).

(2) Notwithstanding this Act or any other enactment, the General Council may make a Policy in respect of all or any of the following:

(a) the prohibition or regulation and control of hunting, killing or taking of wildlife on settlement areas;

(b) the prohibition or regulation and control of trapping on settlement areas;

(c) the prohibition or regulation and control of gathering of wild plants on settlement areas;

(d) subject to any Act of the Parliament of Canada, the prohibition or regulation and control of fishing in settlement areas.

(3) General Council Policies under subsection (2) or an amendment or repeal of them must be approved by all 8 settlement councils and are of no effect unless they are approved by the Lieutenant Governor in Council, which approval may apply to all or any provision of the Policy.

(4) The Lieutenant Governor in Council may,

(a) to protect rare or endangered species, and

(b) after consultation between the Minister and the General Council,

rescind all or any aspect of an approval given under subsection (3) and if that occurs the General Council Policy, or the applicable provision of it is repealed.

(5) If there is a conflict between a General Council Policy approved under this section and this Act or any other enactment, the Policy prevails.

(6) Copies of orders made by the Lieutenant Governor in Council under this section must

(a) be sent to all the settlement councils and the General Council, and

(b) be published in *The Alberta Gazette*.

Schedule 1

s.19 If there is a General Council Policy in effect, a settlement council may, in accordance with that Policy, make by-laws

(a) prohibiting persons who are not settlement members from hunting, trapping, gathering or fishing in the settlement area;

(b) prescribing the terms and conditions under which a person or class of person is permitted to occupy, hunt, trap, gather or fish in the settlement area;

(c) prescribing the manner in which and the terms and conditions subject to which a settlement member may acquire

(i) the right to trap, hunt or gather in the settlement area;

(ii) the right to fish in a marsh, pond, lake, stream or creek in the settlement area and the circumstances under which that right may be suspended, limited or revoked.[309]

Subject to the *Fisheries Act* (Canada) and regulations made thereunder, fishing in settlement areas continues to be restricted to members resident in the settlement areas and persons authorized under settlement by-laws. Members have the right to fish at any time, except spawning season, for sustenance of the member and the member's immediate family, but not for the purpose of selling or dealing in fish. Fishing rights extend to fish in the settlement area and watercourses or bodies of water that actually adjoin the settlement area. Commercial fishing is prohibited without a license issued under the *Fisheries Act* and approved by the settlement council. At the request of a settlement council, the Minister of Forestry, Lands and Wildlife may authorize a council to issue a commercial fishing license. If such licenses are issued, a proportion of the total catch designated by the same Minister must be set aside and made available only for settlement members.[310]

General Council approved a model Hunting, Fishing, Trapping and Gathering By-law in November of 1990 (Appendix 4). The purpose of the bylaw is to "provide for the use, preservation and protection of wildlife, fish and wild plants so that the settlement area will continue to provide a base for traditional Metis pursuits."[311] Hunting, fishing and trapping in the settlement area is limited to licensed members and special permit holders. Gathering is allowed during all seasons. Persons convicted of an offense under the policy may be liable to a fine of up to $2,500. Further, the settlement council may cancel permits and licenses of members convicted of an offense under the policy or the *Wildlife Act*.[312]

# 9

## Broader Legal Context

The Metis settlements legislation is the first provincial legislation to grant collective ownership of land and self-government to an aboriginal people without federal involvement in the negotiation and implementation process. The negotiations focussed on the historical roles assumed by the provincial and federal governments, rather than legal obligations. Although aboriginal rights were asserted in the natural resource litigation and in position papers prepared by the Metis, the driving concern in the negotiations of the new legislation was results.[313] In the end, aboriginal rights language was not included. According to Fred Martin, it was felt that the recognition of aboriginal rights would take the negotiations out of the provincial realm and require participation by the federal government and other provinces in the definition of rights and the constitutional entrenchment of the land base.[314] Further, some settlement members were concerned about the impact of the legislation on their aboriginal rights. As a result, a paragraph was added to the preamble of the *Constitution of Alberta Amendment Act, 1990* to clarify that nothing in the legislation is to be construed so as to abrogate or derogate from aboriginal rights.

Despite the intent not to affect potential Metis aboriginal rights, three important legal questions remain which may affect the legal status of the settlement legislation. These are: Are the Metis "Indians" under s.91(24) of the *Constitution Act, 1867*?; Does the settlements legislation constitute a land claims agreement within the meaning of s.35(3) of the *Constitution Act, 1982*?; Does the absence of aboriginal rights language legitimize the constitutional amending process utilized by the province of Alberta.

### JURISDICTION

The issue of constitutional jurisdiction over Metis peoples is the subject of substantial academic and legal debate but it has yet to be addressed by Canadian courts. Section 91(24) grants jurisdiction over "Indians and lands reserved for the Indians" to the federal government.[315] Although provinces may enact general legislation that has the necessary effect of abrogating aboriginal rights, it cannot pass legislation that singles out Indians for special treatment.[316] The Metis settlements legislation is aimed specifically at Metis peoples as a distinct class of people. If they are s.91(24) Indians, the Metis settlements legislation could be invalid because the province is exercising jurisdiction exclusive to the federal government. In order to avoid this result, one might argue that case law concerning the validity of provincial legislation only addresses the issue of the provincial government passing legislation that has a detrimental effect on aboriginal people. The province may pass legislation for their benefit.[317]

One also has to consider the practical effect of placing jurisdiction in the federal government. It is unlikely that the federal government would unilaterally, and without the consent of the Metis, deprive them of rights recognized by the province nor would a court be quick to recognize this power. Rather, a more likely result is the federal government will endorse the provincial scheme. However, the satisfaction of aboriginal rights claims and the proper process for constitutional entrenchment could be raised before an endorsement is given.

It is clear that the reference to "Indians" in s.91(24) encompasses more than those aboriginal peoples who are included in the federal *Indian Act* regime.[318] An examination of historical records, pre- and post-Confederation statutes, federal political practice and case law can be used to support two contradictory conclusions on the inclusion of Metis peoples under s.91(24): all Metis are s.91(24) Indians or only those who lived the way of life of the Indians and with the Indians are s.91(24) Indians. The contemporary policy of the federal government has been that the Metis peoples south of the 60th parallel are a provincial responsibility. Canada will only pursue limited initiatives with respect to these people through federal spending powers and a recognition of Metis as disadvantaged peoples.[319] With the exception of Alberta, most provinces have maintained that the Metis are a federal responsibility.[320]

In their attempts to address the issue of jurisdiction, academics have taken the approach adopted by the Supreme Court of Canada in the *Eskimo* decision.[321] In this decision historical evidence including official government documents and published texts were relied upon to conclude that Hudson's Bay Company officials, and Canadian and English parliamentarians regarded Eskimos as Indians at the time of Confederation. Of particular influence was a census taken by the Hudson's Bay Select Committee which listed "Esquimaux" under the category of Indians and whites and "half-breeds" together in a separate category. Brian Schwartz argues the exclusion of half-breeds from the Indian category, coupled with oral testimony given in evidence to the Select Committee, supports the conclusion that historically Metis and Indians were considered as two distinct groups of people.[322] On the other hand, Clem Chartier points out ambiguities in the report, passages in the oral testimony, and additional historical evidence that support the opposite conclusion.[323]

Although the *Eskimo* decision did not consider pre-Confederation and post-Confederation legislation, federal practice and case law, these matters would likely be considered if a court was addressing the issue today. The strongest evidence that Metis were considered Indians lies in the recognition of the "half-breed" land claim to Indian title in the *Manitoba Act, 1870*, the *Dominion Lands Acts* of 1879 and 1883, and the option given to Metis people to take treaty or scrip.[324] The scrip distribution system has also been used to support an argument that reference to Indian title in the above constitutional legislation was merely a matter of political expediency. Scrip was also used to satisfy claims of pre-1870 white settlers in the Red River area.[325] Several arguments have been raised to refute this position including: the Metis understood they were to be granted lands assembled into Metis townships and reserves;[326] the fact the same system was used does not mean Metis are not Indians, it just means the process is not unique; the federal government did attempt to set up a half-breed reserve when the scrip system failed (St. Paul des Metis in northern Alberta) and the federal government created separate half-breed reserves under the half-breed adhesion to Treaty No. 3.

The historical evolution of Indian cultures, customary and contemporary rules of membership, reformulation of aboriginal identity by the federal government into classes of status and non-status Indians (that is, no rights under the *Indian Act*) and federal practice suggest that the definition of Indians in s.91(24) may be an evolving definition. It is not one limited by the historical circumstances surrounding s.91(24). This position is supported by the *Eskimo* decision which anticipates a prospective definition by defining Indians as "all present and *future aboriginals* and native subjects of the proposed confederation of British North America."[327] It is also supported by the *Sparrow* decisions which suggests that a generous and liberal interpretation of constitutional provisions is demanded.[328] The new dimensions of the term Indian are reflected in s.35(2) of the *Constitution Act, 1982* which includes Metis in the definition of aboriginal peoples. The fact that the federal government chooses not to exercise its jurisdiction over certain groups of aboriginal peoples does not mean they cease to be s.91(24) Indians. Parliament cannot alter the constitution by legislation or policy.[329]

The powers given to Parliament under s.91(24) are permissive and not mandatory. Consequently, unless there is political will to resolve the grievances of the Metis or the court imposes a legal obligation on the Crown to resolve grievances arising out of its special historical relationship with the aboriginal peoples of Canada, the presumption of federal jurisdiction may not get the Metis any further ahead in the resolution of their claims. Nevertheless, the Metis National Council has pressed the federal government to accept jurisdiction and has called for federal and provincial commitment to negotiate agreements with the Metis.[330] At the same time, the Alberta settlement Metis accepted provincial jurisdiction and prefer to deal directly with the province of Alberta.

The validity and legal obligations of the federal government arising from the scrip distribution system are currently the matter of litigation in Manitoba. The Manitoba Metis litigation alleges that the system adopted was contrary to s.31 of the *Manitoba Act* which intended to protect group rights of the Metis. It also alleges that the Crown breached its fiduciary obligation in the administration of scrip. Alleged breaches include delay, failure to protect s.31 interests, failure to supervise the distribution scheme, failure to provide promised lands, failure to select lands before they were taken by white settlers, and failure to grant lands for the intended purposes.[331] In resolving this issue, the court may address the issue of jurisdiction and Metis aboriginal rights as one of the arguments raised by the Metis is that the *Manitoba Act* is in effect a treaty between the government of Canada and the Metis. On the other hand, the court may link the federal obligation to the specific constitutional provisions at issue rather than to s.91(24) or a general recognition of Metis aboriginal rights. If the Metis in Manitoba are successful, arguments based on the fiduciary obligation of the Crown could be raised by Metis peoples in Alberta who were subject to a similar scrip distribution system.[332]

Arguably, the agreement between the Federation of Metis Settlements and the province of Alberta will not affect claims of the Metis against the federal government arising from aboriginal rights or scrip distribution. However, if the issue is deemed to be one of federal jurisdiction and the Metis are found to have aboriginal rights, this would raise questions as to the validity of the provincial scheme, the legal nature of the agreement reached with the province, and the process adopted for the constitutional protection of the land base. It is unlikely the federal government will endorse the scheme without it being considered as a significant factor in the resolution of Metis aboriginal rights claims.

## SECTION 35(3) OF THE CONSTITUTION

During the litigation, the province and the Metis disagreed on the legal nature of the *Metis Betterment Act* and the rights of Metis peoples. The Metis maintained that the Act was a negotiated scheme that recognized their historical and political rights as aboriginal peoples. The province maintained that the legislation was provincial welfare legislation only. Further, the issue of aboriginal rights was raised by the Metis in the natural resources litigation. The Crown maintained that the only rights the Metis had were those granted by legislation or alternatively, if the Metis had aboriginal rights, these rights were extinguished prior to the enactment of the *Metis Betterment Act* by the scrip distribution system.[333] Although aboriginal rights language appeared in some of the Metis recommendations for new legislation, all reference to aboriginal rights was dropped in the provincial drafts, the Metis Settlements Accord and the present legislation.

The removal of aboriginal rights language caused concern among some Metis who felt the failure to make reference to aboriginal rights could jeopardize the recognition of future rights not addressed in the Accord. Others suggested that a provision relating to aboriginal rights should not be included because an attempt to define aboriginal rights could affect other Metis and the authority of the province to enter into and implement the Accord. The provincial government was not agreeable to addressing aboriginal rights and maintained that the matter was one for the courts.[334] Eventually it was agreed that aboriginal rights would not be addressed.

The problem that arises is whether the intent of the parties and the absence of aboriginal rights language is sufficient to avoid the problem of having the legislation classified as legislation concerned with aboriginal peoples and aboriginal rights. Given that the Metis are recognized as an aboriginal people in the *Constitution Act, 1982*; land entitlement is recognized as an aboriginal right in Canadian law; strong arguments can be made for legal recognition of an aboriginal right to self-government; and, self-government has become an important element in the definition of rights in the political forum, it may be that the lack of express intent and "buzz" words are irrelevant in the classification of the legislation. Further, it should be noted that a condition for the entrenchment of the land base in the Accord (which lead to the legislative package) is that the natural resources trust litigation and "any issues raised in it" would be resolved.[335] The pleadings in the natural resources litigation were amended to remove an aboriginal rights claim prior to the signing of the Accord. Further, *The Constitution of Alberta Amendment Act, 1990*, which entrenched the Metis land base in the constitution of Alberta anticipates the possibility of the land base being protected by the constitution of Canada.[336] The true issue is whether the Metis have aboriginal rights. Assuming they do, the absence of aboriginal rights language may not be an issue in determining the nature of the agreement.

The existence of Metis aboriginal rights raises the question of whether the provincial government has the power to extinguish or regulate aboriginal rights, whether the legislation is entrenched as a land claims agreement in the constitution of Canada and whether the amending procedure adopted by the province to entrench the Metis land base is constitutionally valid. The answer to the first question involves an interpretation of s.91(24) of the *Constitution Act*, 1867 which has already been addressed. However, it should be noted that if s.91(24) encompasses all aboriginal peoples of Canada and federal action, such as scrip distribution, has not effectively extinguished Metis aboriginal rights, strong arguments can be raised to challenge the ability of a province to regulate or extinguish these rights without federal participation.[337]

The answer to the second question requires consideration of several subissues including the capacity of the province of Alberta to enter a land claims agreement, the characteristics of a land claims agreement, the intent of the parties and the extent of potential constitutional protection. If the legislation is a land claims agreement, the Metis settlements legislation, or portions thereof, may be constitutionally entrenched in absence of a special amendment to the constitution of Canada.

In *Sioui* the Supreme Court stated that the capacity of government to enter into a treaty must be seen from the point of view of the Indians negotiating the treaty.[338] The same test could be applied to land claims which are included in the definition of "treaty" for constitutional purposes. Therefore, it is important to determine whether the Federation of Metis Settlements had a reasonable belief in the ability of the province to enter into a land claims agreement.[339] Further, it has been argued that s.35(3) of the constitution has altered the traditional view that only the federal government can enter treaties. The section was included to ensure existing agreements, which involved both the provinces and the federal government, received constitutional protection.[340] Given the agreement of the Federation not to address aboriginal rights, one might conclude in an early stage of the analysis that the agreement is not a land claims agreement. On the other hand, an argument of political expediency could be raised. The uncertain impact of constitutional authority, prior assertion of aboriginal rights and anticipation of entrenchment in the Canadian constitution could support a conclusion that the Metis "recognized the possibility that negotiations with the province could produce constitutionally protected treaty rights."[341]

The Federation and settlement parties were signatories to the Accord. The capacity of the settlement councils and Federation to enter the Accord might be challenged if their authority to negotiate on behalf of the settlement Metis was questionable. However, it is difficult to find support for this argument given the referendum process and the workshops conducted with the settlements prior to the implementation of the legislation.

Drawing again on analogies to treaty law, a valid land claims agreement may be entered into if there is an intention to create legal obligations, a presence of mutually binding obligations, and their are certain measures of solemnity in the signing, the latter factor being important but not determinative.[342] The settlements legislation could pass each of these tests. Of particular significance in the analysis would be the recognition by the settlements that the legislation is intended to resolve the natural resources litigation.

If the legislation is a land claims agreement, the final issue is what provisions of the legislation would be entrenched. Opinions on this issue differ. Some argue the reference to "land" indicates a clear intention that section 35(3) is only intended to entrench provisions in agreements relating to land and land use matters. On the other hand, it has been argued that if the powers of government are analogous to those of a municipal government and the land claim is the principle subject of the agreement, all provisions of the agreement are entrenched.[343] Consequently, it is possible that not only the land base, but all other provisions of the settlements legislation could be constitutionally protected. This would not pose significant difficulties for the province as the legislation maintains a ministerial veto power on General Council Policies unless the veto power is waived by regulation. Arguably, as long as the power has not been waived, the province will continue to have the ultimate say in the governance of settlement lands regardless of whether the legislation is classified as a land claims agreement.

### AMENDING PROCEDURES

As indicated earlier in this book, the *Constitution of Alberta Amendment Act, 1990* amends the constitution of Alberta by confirming the details of the land grant to the Metis in Alberta's constitution until such time as it is protected by the constitution of Canada. Further, the Act provides that the agreement of the General Council is required to amend or repeal the *Metis Settlements Land Protection Act,* to alter or revoke the fee simple title to settlement lands and to dissolve or alter the composition of the Metis Settlements General Council. Section 7 further provides that the Act can only be amended or repealed after a plebescite of settlement members where a majority of the members of each settlement vote in favour of the proposed amendment or repeal.[344] The latter provision is an attempt to provide a procedure which must be followed by the present and future governments of Alberta before the legislation can be changed. In absence of this provision, the provincial legislature has the ability to repeal or amend the legislation unilaterally without the consent of settlement Metis.

The issue of whether the provincial government can bind future governments on matters relating to the procedures by which legislation is to be enacted, amended, or repealed is a controversial issue. The traditional approach to this issue emphasizes the freedom of Parliament and the provincial legislatures to enact or repeal any constitutionally valid legislation. Adopting this approach, a court could conclude that section 7 is not binding on future provincial legislatures thereby leaving the protection of the Metis land base in Alberta's constitution to the political whim of future provincial governments. More contemporary academic opinions support the view that a distinction must be drawn between substance and procedure. While it is clear that attempts by a legislative body to bind its successors on matters of substantive policy will not be effective, there are strong legal arguments to support the conclusion that attempts by one legislative body to bind its successors as to the procedures by which, or the manner and form in which, future legislation is to be enacted, amended or repealed will be binding. If the latter approach is adopted, s.7 arguably binds both the present and future governments of Alberta.[345] One would hope that special consideration will be given to the manner and form of argument given the unique history and constitutional position of the Metis.

It should also be noted that the process adopted to amend the constitution of Alberta is one which presumes that the protection of the Metis land base is purely a provincial matter and that the Metis Settlement Accord only affects the province and the settlements. The authority for the process is adopted from s.45 of the *Constitution Act, 1982* which provides that the legislature of each province may make laws amending the constitution of the province. If the agreement deals with aboriginal rights, it may be argued that this procedure is inappropriate and that the general amendment procedures requiring the consent of all provinces need to be invoked.[346] An argument could be made that aboriginal rights are given protection in the Canadian constitution and that the recognition of Metis aboriginal rights by a province could affect the definition of aboriginal rights in s.35 of the constitution. Although the Metis are an aboriginal people, the history of the provinces and the federal government has been to deny that they have aboriginal rights. The recognition of Metis aboriginal rights and the entrenchment of a land base were issues of discussion in the constitutional conferences required by s.37 of the *Constitution Act, 1982*. Arguably, the recognition of Metis aboriginal rights should be addressed in the definition of aboriginal rights in section 35 and constitutional amendment of that section.

# 10               Conclusion

The Metis settlements legislation represents a significant accomplishment in the resolution of historical grievances between the settlement Metis and the provincial government. Many of the specific problems arising from the administration of the former legislation have been resolved through the goodwill of the province and the Metis and the desire to achieve a practical resolution to Metis grievances. Some of the more significant problems included:

1. The Metis believed that the government had too much control over the continued existence of settlement lands, resource development, administration of trust funds, membership, development, land allocation, and local government. The Metis were in a position of wardship, subject only to an informal policy of devolving more responsibility, dependent completely on the benevolence of the provincial Crown.

2. The government, in the opinion of some, was more concerned with the exploitation of natural resources than the development and well-being of Metis communities.

3. Metis people wanted more control over local government and resources. In particular they wanted control over taxation, community development, regulation of settlement government, membership and traditional economic pursuits.

4. In order to achieve self-government the Metis needed money and under the former regime there were few sources of revenue. They wanted control over all resource revenues and the administration of the trust fund. In the end subsurface resources remained with the Crown, but a substantial financial package was negotiated to settle the natural resources litigation and finance Metis self-government.

5. The legal status of former settlement associations was unclear. As more responsibility devolved to the settlements, status became of increasing importance.

6. The Metis land base was vulnerable. At any time, the province could decide to disestablish a Metis settlement and it had done so contrary to the wishes of settlement members.

Although one might criticize the scheme on the basis of delegated governing powers and the retention of ultimate authority by the provincial Crown, the practice to date in the implementation of the legislation has been one of consultation and cooperation. The system of government becomes vulnerable only when the elements of mutual trust and respect are lost. The entrenchment of the land base, establishment of the Appeal Tribunal and the Co-Management Agreement place significant control over Metis lands in the Metis people, a form of control that many Indian peoples have yet to acquire. In short, the legislation represents a sound practical resolution to Metis grievances and may serve as a model for other aboriginal groups who are able to place trust in the parties with whom they are negotiating.

# Notes

1. *Statutes of Alberta (S.A.)* 1990, c.M-14.8; *S.A.* 1990, c.M-14.3; *S.A.* 1990, c.M-14.5; and *S.A.* 1990, c.22.2.

2. Ibid., *Metis Settlements Act*, Schedule 3.

3. The *Metis Population Betterment Act, S.A.* 1938, c.6 as am. *S.A.* 1940, c.6, s.8(j) provided that with the approval of the Lieutenant Governor in Council, the Minister could by order make regulations which have for their purpose "the advancement and betterment of any Settlement Association, or any members thereof, or the administration of the affairs of any Settlement Association." Pursuant to this provision, Order in Council (O.C.) 1785/43 was promulgated providing for the creation of the Metis Population Betterment Trust Account. This and subsequent regulations provided that various resource revenues were to be paid into the account and administered by the Minister for the benefit of the settlement associations (for example, O.C. 1034/51, O.C. 1244/51 and O.C. 466/60). Legislation in 1979 converted the fund into the Metis Settlements Trust Fund. In 1969 the settlements sued the government for wrongly depositing monies accruing from the sale of natural resources, including petroleum and natural gas, into the provincial treasury but this lawsuit was dismissed on a procedural point. See, *Poitras v. A.G. for Alberta* (1969), 68 W.W.R. 224 (Alta. S.C.). The lawsuit was renewed in 1974 but had yet to go to trial at the time of the settlement legislation negotiations. The province maintained that any rights created under orders in council setting aside settlement areas were limited to the use of the surface. The province did not divest itself of interest in natural resources in the settlement areas, settlement entitlement to resources and proceeds thereof was limited to surface resources only, in the alternative, if the province did divest itself of interests in the settlement area, the disposition excluded mines and minerals. See, *Statement of Defence to Fourth Amended Statement of Claim*, filed in action 83520, Court of Queen's Bench, Judicial District of Edmonton. Surface revenues and money resulting from the co-management of subsurface resource agreements are now paid into the Consolidated Fund created by the *MSA*. See discussion at p. 27 of this book.

4. *Metis Settlements Accord Implementation Act, supra,* note 1, s.50(1). Section 50(2) provides that the condition does not apply if the subject matter referred to in subsection (1) has been "approved by a plebiscite under section 7 of the *Constitution of Alberta Act, 1990.*" The latter Act is discussed at pages 27-28 of this book.

5. In Saskatchewan, eleven farm colonies were formed pursuant to the *Local Improvements District Relief Act, Statutes of Saskatchewan (S.S.)* 1940, c.128 and the *Rehabilitation Act, Revised Statutes of Saskatchewan (R.S.S.)* 1953, c.245. In 1986, title to the Lebret farm was transferred to Lebret Farm Land Foundations Inc. which is owned and operated by Metis and non-status Indians. See, Sask. Indian and Native Affairs Secretariat, news release, "Lebret Farm Transfer to Metis and Non-Status Indians" (18 August 1986). Negotiations for greater control over Metis lands, administration of certain provincial programs and sharing of resource revenues started in 1985 but ended in disagreement in 1987. See D. Purich, *The Metis* (Toronto: James Lorimer, 1988) at 200. In the Northwest Territories the Metis have been unsuccessful in obtaining a satisfactory resolution to their claims and in Manitoba the refusal to recognize the entitlement of Metis peoples to a land base has resulted in litigation before the courts. See, failed

*Dene/Metis Comprehensive Land Claim Agreement in Principle* (Ottawa: Department of Indian Affairs and Northern Development, 1988) and *Dumont et. al. v. A.G. of Canada* (1988) 53 D.L.R. (4th) 25 (Man. C.A.) rev'd (1990). For a general discussion of the Manitoba claim see P. Chartrand, *Manitoba's Metis Settlement Scheme of 1870* (Saskatoon: Native Law Centre, University of Saskatchewan, 1991).

6.  J. Weinstein, *Aboriginal Self-Determination Off A Land Base* (Kingston: Queen's University Institute of Intergovernmental Affairs, 1986) at 45-46.

7.  (U.K.), 30 & 31 Vict., c.3. The issue of whether the provincial government may have exceeded its constitutional legislative powers is discussed in further detail at pages 75-78 of this book.

8.  For example, the Inuit peoples of Canada are not Indians for the purposes of the *Indian Act, Statutes of Canada (S.C.)* 1985, c. 1-6. However, in *Re Eskimo* [1939] S.C.R. 104 the Supreme Court held that the term "Indians" includes the Inuit.

9.  For a discussion of the position of the provincial governments during the First Ministers' Conferences on Aboriginal Constitutional Matters see, R. Dalon, "An Alberta Perspective on Aboriginal Peoples and the Constitution," in M. Boldt and J.A. Long, *The Quest For Justice: Aboriginal Peoples and Aboriginal Rights* (Toronto: University of Toronto Press, 1985) at 111. Some provinces have indicated willingness to negotiate with the Metis on areas of provincial jurisdiction. For example, on the eve of the 1987 constitutional conferences Premier Grant Devine of Saskatchewan indicated his willingness to transfer title to remaining farm colonies to Metis and non-status Indians. More recently, Saskatchewan and Manitoba entered negotiations for devolution of administrative control over provincial services such as education and child welfare. See, Purich, *The Metis, supra,* note 5 at 200.

10. (U.K.), 1982, c.11. Section 35(1) of the constitution provides that existing aboriginal and treaty rights are recognized and affirmed. Section 35(3) clarifies that the reference in s.35(1) to treaty rights includes rights that exist, or may be acquired, by way of modern land claims agreements. Section 35(2) includes Metis people in the definition of the aboriginal peoples of Canada. It is clear that this section was included to satisfy Metis claims to recognition as an aboriginal people, but this was done without prior determination of the existence, nature and scope of Metis rights. See, D. Sanders, "Prior Claims: Aboriginal People in the Constitution of Canada," in S.M. Beck and I. Bernier, eds., *Canada and The New Constitution: The Unfinished Agenda* (Montreal: Institute For Research and Public Policy, 1983) at 232. The issue of whether the settlements legislation constitutes a land claims agreement is discussed in further detail at pages 78-81 of this book.

11. Negotiators were concerned that a reference to aboriginal rights would require an amending process involving all of the provinces as aboriginal rights are not of a purely provincial nature. See, F. Martin, "Federal and Provincial Responsibility in the Metis Settlements of Alberta," in D. Hawkes, ed., *Aboriginal Peoples and Government Responsibility: Exploring Federal and Provincial Roles* (Ottawa: Carleton University Press, 1989) at 278-79.

12. Ibid., at 245.

13. Scrip distribution was authorized under the *Manitoba Act, S.C.* 1870, c.3, s.31 and the *Dominion Lands Acts, S.C.* 1879, c.31, s.125(e) and *S.C.* 1883, c.17, s.81(e) and 83.

14. *Dumont et al. v. A.G. of Canada, supra,* note 5. There are numerous political and academic commentaries on the scrip distribution system. For example, C. Chartier, "Aboriginal Rights and Land Issues: The Metis Perspective," in Boldt and Long, *The Quest For Justice, supra,* note 9 at 55; Chartrand, *Manitoba's Metis Settlement Scheme, supra,* note 5; T. Flanagan, "The Case Against Metis Aboriginal Rights," *Canadian Public*

*Policy* 9, no. 3 (1983): 314-25; J. Sawchuck, P. Sawchuck and T. Ferguson, *Metis Land Rights in Alberta: A Political History* (Edmonton: Metis Association of Alberta, 1981); D. Sanders, "Metis Rights in the Prairie Provinces and the Northwest Territories: A Legal Interpretation," in H. Daniels, *The Forgotten Peoples: Metis and Non-Status Indian Claims* (Ottawa: Native Council of Canada, 1979) at 5-22; D. Sprague "Government Lawlessness in the Administration of Manitoba Land Claims, 1870-1887," *Manitoba Law Journal* 10, no. 4 (1980): 416; and D. Sprague, *Canada and the Metis, 1869-1885* (Waterloo: Wilfrid Laurier Press, 1988).

15. G.F. Stanley, "Alberta's Half-Breed Reserve Saint Paul des Metis 1896-1909," in A.S. Lussier and D.B. Sealey, eds., *The Other Natives: The Metis*, vol. 2 (Winnipeg: Manitoba Metis Federation Press and Editions Bois-Brules, 1978) at 105-7. See also, ibid., Sawchuck et al., *Metis Land Rights in Alberta*, at 172-78.

16. For a summary of scrip distribution under the *Dominion Lands Acts, supra,* note 13 and various provisions of federal Indian legislation see Sanders, "Metis Rights," *supra,* note 14 at 10-13.

17. Purich, *The Metis, supra,* note 5 at 133-34.

18. D. Sanders, "A Legal Analysis of the Ewing Commission and the Metis Colony System in Alberta" (Faculty of Law, University of British Columbia, 1978) [unpublished] at 19, and Alberta Federation of Metis Settlements (AFMS), *Metisism: A Canadian Identity* (Edmonton: Alberta Federation of Metis Settlements, 1982) at 5.

    The Metis National Council holds that the only Metis are members of the Metis Nation and defines its membership as follows:

    > all persons who can show they are descendant of persons considered Metis under the 1870 *Manitoba Act*; all persons who can show they are descendants of Metis under the *Dominion Lands Acts* of 1879 and 1883; and all other persons who can produce proof of aboriginal ancestry and who have been accepted as Metis by the Metis community.

    See, Purich, *The Metis, supra,* note 5 at 13, and Metis National Council, "Statement on Metis Self-Identity," paper presented at the Federal-Provincial Meeting of the First Ministers on Aboriginal Constitutional Matters, Toronto, Ontario, 13-14 February (Doc. 830-143/016).

19. Sawchuk et al., *Metis Land Rights in Alberta, supra,* note 14, at 188.

20. Ibid., at 188-90; Martin, "Federal and Provincial Responsibility," *supra,* note 11 at 255. The Commission's mandate was with respect to the "half-breed" population of Alberta. At page 4 of the Commission's report, the Commission explains:

    > It may be well to define here the term "half-breed" or "Metis." ... By either term is meant a person of mixed blood, white and Indian, who lives the life of the ordinary Indian, and includes non-treaty Indian. It is apparent to everyone that there are in this province many persons of mixed blood (Indian and white) who have settled down as farmers, who are making a good living in that occupation and do not need, nor do they desire, public assistance. The term as used in this report has no application to such men.

21. Alberta, "Report of the Ewing Commission" (Commissioner: Honourable A.F. Ewing), in Native Affairs Secretariat, *Alberta's Metis Settlements: A Compendium of Background Documents* (Alberta: Policy and Planning Division, 1984), section 3 at 3.

22. In the opinion of the Commission, the Metis population in the north was landless, poverty stricken, under-educated and disease ridden. See ibid., at 2-8.

23. Ibid., at 13.

24. D. Sanders, "A Legal Analysis of the Ewing Commission," *supra*, note 18 at 21. For a general discussion of the Ewing Commission see Martin, "Federal and Provincial Responsibility," *supra*, note 11 at 256-61; T.C. Pocklington, *The Government and Politics of the Alberta Metis Settlements* (Regina: Canadian Plains Research Center, 1991) at 12-21; and Sawchuk et al., *Metis Land Rights in Alberta, supra*, note 14 at 190-96.

25. The *Metis Population Betterment Act*, later called the *Metis Betterment Act*, S.A. 1938, c.6.

26. Ibid., s.2(a).

27. See Appendix 1.

28. Martin, "Federal and Provincial Responsibility," *supra*, note 11 at 263. For a general discussion of the evolution of Metis legislation see also Pocklington, *Government and Politics, supra*, note 24 at 24-44; Sawchuk et al., *Metis Land Rights in Alberta, supra*, note 14 at 196-212; and K. Young, "Alberta's Metis Settlement Legislation: A Legislative History," *Legal Information Service*, no. 17 (Saskatoon: Native Law Centre, University of Saskatchewan).

29. *S.A.* 1940, c.6, s.8.

30. Ibid., sections 8, 9, 14, and 18.

31. Ibid., s.4(2).

32. *S.A.* 1952, c.6, s.2 amending ibid., s.4(2). Inconsistencies between the legislation and regulations rendered this section unworkable over time resulting in the provision being largely ignored by the government and Metis. Instead, in practice the election procedure was reintroduced and maintained. See, Martin, "Federal and Provincial Responsibility," *supra*, note 11 at 264-65 and 269; Young, "Alberta's Metis Settlement Legislation," *supra*, note 28 at 10.

33. Pocklington, *Government and Politics, supra*, note 24 at 27.

34. *Supra*, note 3.

35. Martin, "Federal and Provincial Responsibility," *supra*, note 11 at 269-71.

36. Ibid., and Young, "Alberta's Metis Settlement Legislation," *supra*, note 28 at 9.

37. "The Report of The Metis Task Force Upon the *Metis Betterment Act*, Metis Settlements and the Metis Rehabilitation Branch" (chair: T.F. Roach), in *Alberta's Metis Settlements, supra*, note 21, section 8.

38. Ibid., at 9

39. Ibid., at 10-11.

40. Martin, "Federal and Provincial Responsibility," *supra*, note 11 at 270.

41. O.C. 422/82, Appendix 1 in Alberta, *Foundations For the Future of Alberta's Metis Settlements: Report of the MacEwan Joint Committee on the Metis Betterment Act and Regulations* (chair: Dr. G. MacEwan) (Edmonton: 1984). For a general discussion see Pocklington, *Government and Politics, supra*, note 24 at 141.

42. *Supra*, note 10, s.37. Existing aboriginal and treaty rights were left undefined in the constitution on the assumption that these issues would be clarified through a series of constitutional conferences. Metis right, the right to a land base and self-government were topics of discussion. However, the First Ministers and national aboriginal representatives were unable to reach agreement on these and other matters leaving them to be addressed by the courts.

43. *Supra*, note 18.

44. AFMS, *By Means of Conferences and Negotiations We Ensure Our Rights* (Edmonton: Alberta Federation of Metis Settlement Associations, 1986) at 5.

45. AFMS, *Metisism, supra,* note 18 at 57. For a general discussion see Pocklington, *Government and Politics, supra,* note 24 at 138-41.

46. *Poitras* v. *A.G. for Alberta, supra,* note 3 at 235.

47. AFMS, *Metisism, supra,* note 18 at 17 and 47.

48. *Fourth Amended Statement of Claim* and *Statement of Defence to Fourth Amended Statement of Claim, supra,* note 3. The issue of Metis aboriginal rights has yet to be raised before the courts and has received little academic treatment. See for example, *supra,* note 14; C. Bell, "Metis Aboriginal Title" (L.L.M. Thesis, University of British Columbia, 1989) and Native Council of Canada, A *Statement of Claim Based on Aboriginal Title of the Metis and Non-Status Indians* (Ottawa: Native Council of Canada, 1980).

49. AFMS, *Metisism, supra,* note 18 at 29.

50. AFMS, *By Means of Conferences and Negotiations, supra,* note 44 at 1.

51. Pursuant to the *Indian Act, supra,* note 8, the federal government holds legal title to reserve lands for the use and benefit of Indian bands. A usufruct is the right to use, enjoy and profit from property, the legal ownership of which is vested in another.

52. AFMS, *Metisism, supra,* note 18 at 57-63.

53. *Statement of Defence to Fourth Amended Statement of Claim, supra,* note 3.

54. AFMS, *Metisism, supra,* note 18 at 7.

55. The Metis apparently prepared drafts of the enabling legislation and worked with the government on subsequent revisions until the final draft was completed. See Sawchuck et al., *Metis Land Rights in Alberta, supra,* note 14 at 198 and Martin, "Federal and Provincial Responsibility," *supra,* note 11 at 261-62.

56. *Supra,* note 25.

57. *Supra,* note 53.

58. *Supra,* note 41, at 4-8.

59. Ibid., Appendix 1.

60. Ibid., at 11 and 59.

61. Ibid., Appendix 2.

62. *Supra,* note 41 at 59.

63. *Local Authorities Election Act, Revised Statutes of Alberta,* (R.S.A.) 1980, c.L-27.5.

64. *Supra,* note 41 at 24.

65. Ibid., at 59-60.

66. Ibid., at 56-57. These matters have also been excluded from the 1990 settlements legislation. However, they are addressed in a framework agreement between the Metis Association of Alberta, which represents various Metis local organizations throughout the province, and the province of Alberta. The agreement requires the establishment of a joint committee to plan the course of action under the agreement. Specific agreements have been reached through the consultation process created by the framework agreement and administrative agencies such as the Metis Children's Services Society of Edmonton have been created.

67. *Supra* note 41 at 11.

68. Martin, "Federal and Provincial Responsibility," *supra,* note 11 at 273.

69. Dalon, "An Alberta Perspective," *supra,* note 9 at 91, 106 and 111.

70. Originally the *Alberta Act*, 1905, 4-5 Edw. VII, c.3, now identified as part of the constitution of Canada by s.52(2)b of the *Constitution Act, 1982, supra*, note 10.

71. Alberta, Legislative Assembly, *A Resolution Concerning an Amendment to the Alberta Act*, No. 18 (3 June 1985) in Alberta, *Implementation of Resolution 18 (A Resolution Concerning an Amendment to the Alberta Act)* (Edmonton: Alberta Municipal Affairs) at 2-4.

72. Ibid.

73. Martin, "Federal and Provincial Responsibility," *supra*, note 11 at 276.

74. AFMS, *By Means of Conferences and Negotiations, supra*, note 44.

75. Ibid., at 16.

76. Ibid., at 20-32 and 34-44.

77. Ibid., at 32-34 and 64-68.

78. Ibid., at 51 and 71-72.

79. R.S.A. 1980, c.L-5.

80. AFMS, *By Means of Conferences and Negotiations, supra*, note 44 at 50-58.

81. Pocklington, *Government and Politics, supra*, note 24 at 147-50.

82. 3d. Sess, 21st Leg. Alta, 1988.

83. Pocklington, *Government and Politics, supra*, note 24 at 149.

84. Martin, "Federal and Provincial Responsibility," *supra*, note 11 at 275.

85. Ibid., at 276.

86. *Supra*, note 82, ss.2 and 3.

87. Ibid., ss.4-43.

88. Ibid., ss.13-16 and 69.

89. Martin, "Federal and Provincial Responsibility," *supra*, note 85.

90. *Supra*, note 82, ss.44-61.

91. Ibid., s.55.

92. Ibid., s.64.

93. Ibid., ss.77 and 87-91.

94. Ibid., ss.78-83.

95. Pocklington, *Government and Politics, supra*, note 24 at 149.

96. Ibid., at 150-51.

97. Ibid at 151.

98. Some controversy arose in November of 1989 when Paddle Prairie pulled out of the Accord. Concern was expressed over the powers of General Council (formerly Okimawiwin), the equal distribution of funds among settlements regardless of their populations and relative expenses, and the potential abrogation of aboriginal rights. In April 1990 Attorney General Ken Rostad ordered that the chair of Paddle Prairie step down in order to resolve a deadlock on Council regarding membership in the Federation and participation in the Accord. Paddle Prairie opted to remain a party to the Accord and issues of concern were addressed in subsequent negotiations. Of particular interest is the preamble of the *Constitution of Alberta Amendment Act, 1990, supra*, note 10 which provides that nothing in the legislation is to be construed so as to abrogate or derogate from any aboriginal rights referred to in s.35 of the constitution.

For a discussion of the Paddle Prairie pullout see J. Holman and D. Wagg, "Paddle Prairie Pulls Out of Federation," *Windspeaker*, 24 November 1989, 1-2; J. Holman, "Paddle Prairie Residents Vote No to Pullout," *Windspeaker*, 26 January 1990, 1-2; J. Holman, Paddle Prairie Resident Files Lawsuit to Declare Referendum Illegal," *Windspeaker*, 16 January 1990, 1-2; and D. Thomas, "Metis Chair Fighting Dismissal," *Edmonton Journal*, 12 April 1990.

99. 2d. Sess., 22nd Leg. Alta., 1990.

100. *Supra*, note 1.

101. Ibid., ss.50-51.

102. Ibid., by-law authority is specified in Schedule 1 of the *Metis Settlements Act*.

103. Ibid., ss.52-55. In an emergency that affects the health or safety of the community, the settlement council may decide, by unanimous resolution, that a public meeting and vote are not required. See ibid., s.56.

104. Ibid., ss.74-98 and Metis Settlements General Council Land Policy (G.C.P. 90003), *Alberta Gazette*, 1992, I.2592 (draft 09/12/91), part 4.

105. Ibid., s.72, 227(c) and 249. By-laws no longer need to be approved by the Minister as the three-year period has now expired. They must still conform to General Council Policy.

106. Ibid., ss.214-232.

107. Ibid., s.226. Minister is defined in the Act as the member of Executive Council responsible for the administration of the Act. For a detailed discussion of settlement government see Pocklington, *Government and Politics, supra*, note 24.

108. Ibid., ss.180-213. For a general discussion of the composition and jurisdiction of the panels see *Metis Settlements Appeals Tribunal* (Edmonton: Metis Settlements Appeals Tribunal, 1991). The author is currently working on a book which will examine the operations and decisions of the Tribunal from 1990-1995. The book is expected to be released in 1997. Decisions of the Tribunal can be obtained from the Tribunal office in Edmonton.

109. Alberta Regulation 337/90.

110. Ibid., ss.10-13.

111. See, *supra*, note 1, ss.74-98 and 234.

112. Ibid., s.1(j).

113. Ibid., s.75. Eligibility criteria for membership under the *MSA* do not apply to the Transitional Membership Regulation. The adoption of Indians as members of the settlements through the Regulation is a political issue with settlement residents and the Metis Nation of Alberta.

114. A sample letters patent is attached as Appendix 2. Fee simple title is the greatest interest a person can acquire in land. Letters patent are instruments issued by the Lieutenant Governor in Council granting a right or interest in land. The concept of fee simple is discussed in further detail at pages 34-35 of this book.

115. *Supra*, note 1, ss.111-129. Resource management and surface access are discussed in further detail at pages 66-72 of this book.

116. Ibid., s.99.

117. Ibid., s.99 and 222.

118. *Supra*, note 104.

119. Ibid., s.1.2.

120. Land Interests Conversion Regulation, Alberta Regulation 362/91.

121. Ibid., s.104.

122. Ibid., s.102; Metis Settlements Land Registry Regulation, Alberta Regulation 361/91.

123. Joint Land Committee, *Renovating The Foundation: Proposals For A Model Land Recording and Registration Act For The Provinces and Territories of Canada* (Edmonton: Alberta Law Reform Institute, 1990).

124. The initial proposal for the establishment of the Transition Commission contained in the Accord provides that the Commission should be structured in a flexible manner in accordance with the principle that "form follows function" and that the Commission be "staffed, *as far as possible*, by personnel from settlement organizations and government departments and agencies currently serving the settlements" [emphasis added]. See, *Settlements Accord* made on 1 July 1989 between the Government of Alberta and the Alberta Federation of Metis Settlements at 7. As a matter of policy the Commission is facilitating professional development through on-the-job training and has hired approximately one-third of the Commission staff from the settlements.

125. Payments of money out of Part 2 of the Consolidated Fund are severely restricted and are not subject to payment out in accordance with General Council Policy until 1 April 2007. In essence, Part 2 operates a secure reserve fund for the settlements. See, *Metis Settlements Act, supra*, note 1, s.142(2).

126. Government of Alberta news release (1 November 1990) quoted in L. MacLachlan, "The 1990 Alberta Metis Settlements Legislation: An Overview," *Resources* (winter 1991).

127. *Supra*, note 4.

128. *Supra*, note 1.

129. Registry Regulation, *supra*, note 122, s.3(1).

130. *Metis Settlements Act, supra*, note 1, s.103.

131. Recording refers to the making of a record and the making of an entry of a document, or copy, on a register. It is the administrative process through which entries in a register confer priority and enforcement of an interest. Registration also refers to the making of an entry on the register which confers both priority and confirms or terminates ownership interests. See, Registry Regulation, *supra*, note 122, ss.1(l) and 1(o) and *Model Land Recording and Registration Act, supra*, note 123 at 8-9.

132. For a discussion of the problems associated with the Indian Lands Registry see P.J. Clark, "Registration of Interests in Indian Lands," in *Indians and the Law* (Vancouver: Continuing Legal Education Society of British Columbia, 1982).

133. *Supra*, note 123.

134. *Supra*, note 121. Those provisions which are incorporated relate to implied covenants, grants of easements and restrictive covenants, utility interests, party wall agreements, encroachment agreements, cancellation of certain interest leases, recording of writs, and sales made under process of law. See, Registry Regulation, *supra*, note 122, part 9.

135. For a discussion of the fundamental elements of the torrens system of registration upon which the Model Act and *Registry Regulation* are based see, T. Mapp, *Torrens' Elusive Title*, Alberta Law Review Book Series, vol. 1 (Edmonton: Alberta Law Review, 1978), ch. 4.

136. *Supra*, note 131.

137. Registry Regulation, *supra*, note 122, ss.6-11.

138. Ibid., s.11.

139. Ibid., s.1(h) of the Registry Regulation, defines an interest as "the fee simple estate in patented land and a right or interest in the fee simple referred to in s.99 of the [*Metis Settlements*] *Act*."

140. Ibid., document is defined in s.1(f) of the Registry Regulation and includes plans, maps and "any information that can be converted by a machine or device into a form that people can read."

141. Ibid., ss.82-91.

142. Ibid., s.16.

143. Ibid., s.18-21.

144. Ibid., s.26.

145. See also, Land Policy, *supra*, note 104, s.2.12.

146. *Supra*, note 122, ss.31-35.

147. Ibid., ss.37-44.

148. Ibid., s.76.

149. *Supra*, note 122.

150. Ibid., ss.94-108.

151. The use of the word "only" in s.99 could give rise to an argument that the common law of property does not apply and that the only rights and interest in land are those created pursuant to s.99. However, several arguments can be raised against this interpretation. First, it is a general rule of statutory interpretation that exclusion of the common law must be explicit or necessarily inconsistent with the operation of the legislation. Second, it would be an impractical and impossible task to legislate the entire common law of property through legislation. Third, the Land Policy is intended to provide a framework for ownership and management of settlement lands. Several provisions in the Land Policy and the Registry Regulation suggest they are not intended to be an exhaustive statutory expression of land law concerning the creation, nature, recognition and registration of rights and interests in settlement land. Finally, the adoption of general framework policy and the decision not to articulate an exhaustive list of rights could result in harsh results if principles of common law or analogous principles were excluded.

152. Mapp, *Torrens' Elusive Title, supra*, note 135 at 17.

153. An example of express abolition of equity can be found in s.2(2) of the Registry Regulation, *supra*, note 122 which provides:

    The equitable doctrine variously known as "notice" and "constructive notice" is abolished for the purpose of determining if conduct is fraudulent under this Regulation.

154. *R.S.A.* 1980, c.A-1; *R.S.A.* 1980, c.D-34; and *R.S.A.* 1980, c.W-1.

155. *R.S.A.* 1980, c.W-5; *R.S.A.* 1980, c.L-15; *R.S.A.* 1980, c.L-6; *R.S.A.* 1980, c.P-30; *R.S.A.* 1980, c.D-38; *R.S.A.* 1980, c.M-9; *R.S.A.* 1980, c.I-9; and *R.S.A.* 1980, c.V-1.

156. *Supra*, note 1. The specific reservations and conditions placed on the grant of title to the General Council are specified in the letters patent issued by the Province of Alberta to General Council on 1 November 1990, in relation to each of the eight settlement areas.

157. *Supra*, note 120.

158. Ibid., ss.3 and 14.

159. Land Policy, *supra*, note 104, s.2.13 and Registry Regulation, *supra*, note 122, s.9.

160. Ibid., Registry Regulation, s.16(8).

161. Ibid., s.1(g) and *Metis Settlements Act, supra*. note 1, s.253.

162. Ibid., Registry Regulation, ss.16(7) and 110.

163. Land Policy, *supra*, note 104, ss.2.2, 2.3; *Metis Settlements Act, supra*, note 1, s.2(1) and the Registry Regulation, *supra*, note 122, s.29(2). The provisions in the Land Policy suggest that the settlement corporation is the person in law entitled to Metis title in the event that a condition to the grant of title is not met. The title would be held in trust until the Appeal Tribunal or the court rendered a decision on the entitlement of the person registered to hold Metis title.

164. *Supra*, note 104. (See Appendix 4 re. copy of the form for Provisional Metis Title.)

165. *Metis Settlements Act, supra*, note 1, s.101.

166. This conclusion is drawn from references to the fee simple in the singular, the creation of a category of interests "less than the fee simple estate in patented land," and the creation of two distinct registers for the fee simple estate and Metis title.

167. *Supra*, note 104. (See Appendix 6 re. copy of the form for Provisional Metis Title.)

168. Land Policy, *supra*, note 104, ss.4.1-4-5, 4.7 and 5.2.

169. Some confusion may arise in the interpretation of the Land Policy and Registry Regulation as provisions dealing with leases do not expressly exclude application to provisional Metis title and allotments. Of particular concern are implied terms of commercial leases which could apply to allotments made for commercial purposes. Implied terms of leases are discussed in further detail at pages 44-46.

170. A reversionary interest is simply defined as a right to future enjoyment of property presently in the possession or occupation of another.

171. A forfeiture may arise and the tenancy determined upon breach of a condition of a lease. The landlord has the right to terminate the lease and resume possession even if this right is not expressed. Whether or not the right is expressed, the court will be construed strictly against the landlord. In certain circumstances, including hardship to the defendant, a court may grant relief to the tenant rather than end the tenancy. Such relief will not be granted where breach is willful.

172. Land Policy, *supra*, note 104, ss.2.6 and 4.1-4.7.

173. *Supra*, note 104. (See Appendix 7 re. copy of the form for Memorandum of Allotment.)

174. Ibid., s.3.4.

175. Ibid., s.5.2.

176. Ibid., s.2.8 and 3.3.

177. Ibid., s.2.9 and 2.10.

178. *Supra*, note 165 and Land Policy, *supra*, note 4, s.2.12.

179. Land Policy, *supra*, note 104, s.3.6.

180. A constructive trust is a relationship with respect to property subjecting the person by whom the property is held to the equitable interests of someone else. The primary concern of the court is the title holder would be unjustly enriched if permitted to retain the property.

181. Land Policy, *supra*, note 104, ss.6.1-6.4.

182. *Metis Settlements Act, supra,* note 1, s.108.

183. Land Policy, *supra,* note 104, ss.3.2 and 2.11; Metis Settlement General Council Timber Policy (GC 90002), *Alberta Gazette,* 1991, I.1760.

184. Ibid., s.3.7.

185. See terms of letters patent for settlement areas, Appendix 2 of this book.

186. Ibid., ss.1.3 and 2.7 and Registry Regulation, *supra,* note 122, ss.8(1)(b), 80 and 81.

187. *Supra,* note 176.

188. Land Policy, *supra,* note 104, s.3.5.

189. Ibid.

190. *Supra,* note 171.

191. Land Policy, *supra,* note 104, ss.2.9, 2.10, 2.11, and 3.7.

192. *Supra,* note 164.

193. Riparian rights are discussed in further detail below. A riparian owner is a person who owns property abutting upon a body of water.

194. An easement is a right of use over the property of another. The term is normally used to refer to rights of use attributed to adjoining lands. The benefit of the right of use is attached to the land, rather than a specific individual who owns or occupies the land. The land having the right of use is known as the dominant tenement and the land which is subject to the easement is known as the servient tenement. A prescriptive easement is one which is a right to use a way, water, light or air by reason of continuous usage.

195. *Supra,* note 155.

196. *Didow* v. *Knox* (1988) A.R. 250 (C.A).

197. *Supra,* note 104 at note 11.

198. *Supra,* note 122, s.36

199. *Supra,* note 123.

200. Ibid., at 27.

201. Ibid.

202. See, D. Percy, "Water Rights in Alberta," *Alberta Law Review* 15 (1977): 142.

203. Ibid., at 143 and 157.

204. *Water Resources Act, supra,* note 155, s.1(g).

205. *Supra,* note 202 at 157.

206. *Supra,* note 155.

207. Freehold estates are estates in land of uncertain duration. Today these include the fee simple and life estates. Life estates may be for the duration of the life of the holder of the estate or the life of some other person. Freeholds are contrasted to leaseholds which are estates of certain duration or of a duration that is capable of being rendered certain.

208. Several problems in the application of the *Dower Act, supra,* note 155 are discussed in the following pages. Of particular concern is the fact that Metis title is a unique statutory interest not contemplated by the *Dower Act.* If the *Dower Act* does not apply, the common law may not apply either because it has been abolished by legislation. The result is Metis land may not be subject to dower rights.

209. Land Policy, *supra*, note 104, s.7.3.

210. Ibid., s.7.2. The definition of homestead in s.1(e) the *Dower Act, supra*, note 155, also places territorial limits on the extent of the homestead. It cannot consist of more than four adjoining lots in one block in a city, town or village and not more than one quarter section of land other than land in a city, town or village. The certificate of Metis title is limited to a maximum of two quarter sections and one hamlet lot, but additional lands may be acquired by allotment.

211. Ibid., ss.7.3(2) and (3).

212. *Supra*, note 1, ss.92 and 93.

213. H. Black, *Black's Law Dictionary*, 5th ed. (St. Paul, MN: West Publishing Co., 1979) at 1176.

214. *Supra*, note 104, s.7.2.

215. *Supra*, note 155, s.23.

216. Ibid., s.1(d).

217. Ibid., ss.1(c) and (d).

218. *Supra*, note 122, s.80.

219. For example, the action for damages for disposition without consent arises upon registration of the wrongful disposition at the provincial Land Titles Office. Provisions providing for the registration of dispositions, orders dispensing with consent, affidavits by the transferor that he or she is not married, and Certificate of Acknowledgement all presume registration with the Registrar of Land Titles.

220. *Supra*, note 155.

221. Ibid.

222. *Supra*, note 79.

223. *Supra*, note 1.

224. *Supra*, note 155, s.1(f).

225. Ibid., s.2(4).

226. Ibid., s.2. The *Landlord and Tenant Act* is currently being revised and may at a future date be nonapplicable to commercial tenancies.

227. *Supra*, note 79.

228. *Supra*, note 173.

229. Ibid., s.7.5.

230. Ibid., s.7.6.

231. Ibid., s.7.2.

232. Ibid., s.7.8.

233. *Supra*, note 230.

234. *Supra*, note 231.

235. Ibid., ss.7.9 and 7.10.

236. Ibid., s.7.11.

237. Ibid.

238. Ibid., ss.7.12 and 7.13.

239. *R.S.A.* 1985, c.P-9. Other legislation that may affect land use planning includes legislation that allows annexation of land by a municipality such as the *Municipal Government Act, R.S.A.* 1980, c.M-26, s.26. Other relevant legislation includes the *Uniform Building Standards Act, R.S.A.* 1980, c.U-4; environmental legislation; the *Public Health Act, S.A.* 1984, c.P-27.1; the *Public Highways Development Act, R.S.A.* 1980, P-28; and the *Historical Resources Act, R.S.A.,* c.H-8. Under s.108 of the *Metis Settlements Act, supra,* note 1, the settlement may expropriate land for the purpose of the settlement. Sections 283 and 284 of the *MSA* outline consequential amendments to the *Public Health Act* and *Public Highways Development Act* so that this legislation will apply to settlement councils and the settlement areas. The *Uniform Building Standards Act* and *Historical Resources Act* ( prohibits development and certain use of designated historic and culturally significant sites) are not specifically addressed and therefore apply.

240. Ibid., s.280.

241. Ibid., s.255.

242. F. Laux, *Planning Law and Practice in Alberta* (Toronto: Carswell, 1990) at 42.

243. For further details on the powers of these planning agencies see, ibid., at 42-49.

244. For further information see, ibid., at 49-58.

245. For example, regional planning could affect the migration of wildlife around and in the settlement area.

246. *Metis Settlements Act, supra,* note 1 at s.110.

247. Ibid., s.107. See Alberta Regulation 363/91.

248. Ibid., ss.224 and 225.

249. Ibid., ss.249 and 250.

250. Ibid., s.223(e).

251. For example, application for allotments may not be approved if the land is not used for farming, ranching, or operating a business.

252. Subdivision Regulation, *supra,* note 247, s.5.

253. *Metis Settlements Act, supra,* note 1, s.18 and schedule 1.

254. Ibid., ss.65-71.

255. Ibid., s.21.

256. Ibid., s.253.

257. Ibid., ss.9, 12, 13 and 15. See also Laux, *Planning Law and Practice in Alberta, supra,* note 242 at 52-53.

258. Ibid., s.108.

259. *Supra,* note 104, s.8.1. For a discussion of the limitation placed on the Tribunal's jurisdiction under this section by the Alberta Court of Appeal see p. 24 of this book.

260. Registry Regulation, *supra,* note 122, s.12.

261. *Supra,* note 1, s.189.

262. Ibid., s.204.

263. *Metis Settlements Accord Implementation Act, supra,* note 1, s.12.

264. *Supra,* note 1, ss.105 and 106.

265. *Supra,* note 242 at 52.

266. *Supra,* note 247.

267. *Supra*, note 1, ss.105 and 106.

268. *Supra*, note 242 at 317.

269. A "parcel" means "the land described in a Metis title register or a register for provisional Metis title, and allotment or a leasehold established under the Registry Regulation," *supra*, note 122.

270. Subdivision Regulation, *supra*, note 247, s.1(2).

271. Ibid., ss. 3, 6-8, 9(2) and 11.

272. Ibid., s.9(1)(b). Broad discretion would allow the Commissioner to disallow a subdivision if the intended use was considered hazardous and to determine the appropriate location of certain developments and uses such as sewage lagoons and sour gas facilities.

273. Ibid., ss.9(3)and (4), 10, 13 and 14(1)-(3).

274. Ibid., s.14(3).

275. Registry Regulation, *supra*, note 122, ss.81-90.

276. Subdivision Regulation, *supra*, note 247, ss.11, 12 and 14(2).

277. Registry Regulation, *supra*, note 122, s.90. See also, *supra*, note 259.

278. *Metis Settlements Act, supra*, note 1, ss.186, 187 and 288.

279. L. MacLachlan, "The 1990 Alberta Metis Settlements Legislation: An Overview," details on resource management provisions (10 January 1991) [unpublished] at 6.

280. Ibid.

281. *Supra*, note 1, s.129.

282. Ibid., s.101(n)(o).

283. Ibid., ss.186 and 187.

284. Ibid., ss.114(2) and 253. Section 11(e) defines an existing mineral lease as the right to work or develop minerals at the date the legislation comes into force.

285. *Supra*, note 104, s.2.11.

286. *Metis Settlements Act, supra*, note 1, ss.115-118.

287. Ibid., ss.122 and 204.

288. Ibid., s.114(2).

289. Ibid., ss.111(a) and 114(2); *Metis Settlements Land Protection Act, supra*, note 1, s.7.

290. *Supra*, note 286.

291. Ibid., s.120.

292. Ibid., ss.119, 120 and 123-128.

293. Ibid., s.111(j).

294. *Supra*, note 1.

295. Ibid., ss.111(h), 119 and 121.

296. Ibid., ss.123-125.

297. Ibid., s.111(d); MacLachlan, "The 1990 Alberta Metis Settlements," *supra*, note 279 at 5.

298. Ibid., s.101(k) of the *Metis Settlements Act* defines minerals as follows:

> "Minerals" means the whole or any part of the mines and minerals, as defined in

the *Mines and Minerals Act,* owned by the Minister in the whole or any part of the Metis Settlements Lands, that are not subject to a Disposition

(i) that was issued by the Minister before the Effective date [of the Agreement], or

(ii) that is issued by the Minister after the Effective Date but that arises out of, or that is a renewal, continuation, reinstatement or other like extension under the Act of any Disposition issued before the effective date.

299. Ibid., ss.101(l), (p), (s) and 201-302.

300. Ibid., s.303.

301. Ibid., ss.304-310.

302. Ibid., ss.501-505.

303. *S.A.* 1987, c.W-9.1.

304. *Supra,* note 25, s.7.

305. *R.S.C.* 1985, c.M-7.

306. Martin, "Federal and Provincial Responsibility," *supra,* note 11 at 282.

307. Ibid., at 281-82.

308. *Supra,* note 105.

309. *Supra,* note 1.

310. Ibid., ss.130-133. See also, *Alberta Fisheries Regulations, C.R.C.* 1978, c.838.

311. Hunting, Fishing, Trapping, Gathering Policy (GC 90001), O.C. 642/90, *Alberta Gazette,* 1991, I.1719, s.1.1.

312. *Supra,* note 303.

313. Martin, "Federal and Provincial Responsibility," *supra,* note 11 at 245.

314. Ibid., at 278. Many Metis settlement members were also concerned that the legislation would affect their aboriginal rights. See, for example, discussion at page 20 of this book.

315. *Supra,* note 7.

316. *R.* v. *Dick* [1985] S.C.R. 309.

317. See for example, A. Pratt, "Federalism in the Era of Aboriginal Self-Government," in Hawkes, *Aboriginal Peoples and Government Responsibility* at 53.

318. For example, *Re Eskimo, supra,* note 8.

319. In attempts to get support for 1990 constitutional proposals Prime Minister Mulroney, for the first time, referred to the Metis as a Nation and indicated a willingness to negotiate with them and the provinces pursuant to the proposed constitutional arrangements for negotiating self-government.

320. *Supra,* note 9.

321. *Supra,* note 8.

322. B. Schwartz, *First Principles: Constitutional Reform With Respect To the Aboriginal Peoples of Canada,1982-1984* (Kingston, Queen's University Institute of Intergovernmental Relations, 1985) at 205-10.

323. C. Chartier, "Indians: An Analysis of the Term Used in Section 91(24) of the British North America Act, 1867," *Saskatchewan Law Review* 43 (1978-79): 42-49.

324. *S.C.* 1870, c.3, s.31; 42 Vict. c.31, s.125(e) and 46 Vict. c.17, s.81 and 83. Of particular interest is the half-breed adhesion to Treaty No. 3. They negotiated separately from the Indians and had separate reserves allotted to them but in 1876 they were forced to join a nearby band. As the treaty negotiation process extended into what is now Alberta and Saskatchewan, half-breeds had the option to declare themselves Indians and take treaty or alternatively to take scrip. See for example, A. Morris, *The Treaties of Canada with the Indians of Manitoba and the Northwest Territories* (Toronto: Bedford, Clark, 1880) at 294-95, and J. Foster, "The Metis: The People and the Term," *Prairie Forum* 3, no. 1 (1978): 83.

325. Schwartz, *First Principles, supra,* note 322 at 222, and T. Flanagan, "Case Against Metis Aboriginal Rights," *supra,* note 14.

326. This argument is raised by counsel for the Metis and accepted by the dissent in *Dumont* v. *A.G. of Canada and the A.G. of Manitoba* (1988) 52 D.L.R. (4th) 25 (M.C.A.). The Supreme Court of Canada reversed the Court of Appeal's decision that Metis claims arising out of s.31 were nonjusticiable. The matter has yet to go to trial.

327. *Supra,* note 8 at 118, 119 and 121 (emphasis added).

328. (1990), 70 D.L.R. 385 (S.C.C.).

329. K. Lysyk, "The Unique Constitutional Position of the Indians," *Canadian Bar Review* 45 (1967): 515.

330. C. Chartier, *In the Best Interest of the Metis Child* (Saskatoon: University of Saskatchewan Native Law Centre, 1988) at 47-48.

331. *Dumont, supra,* note 5. For an excellent discussion of the claim see Chartrand, *Manitoba's Metis Settlement Scheme,* and D.N. Sprague, *supra,* note 14.

332. The treaty argument would likely not be available as the Metis did not negotiate the provisions in the *Dominion Lands Acts, supra,* note 324. However, arguments relating to the recognition of aboriginal rights and the fiduciary obligation of the federal government could be raised.

333. *Supra,* note 55.

334. Martin, "Federal and Provincial Responsibility," *supra,* note 11 at 279, and S. Enge, "Rights Clause Wanted," *Windspeaker,* 9 June 1989, 1.

335. See preamble to the Alberta-Metis Settlements Accord (1 July 1989).

336. *Supra,* note 1, s.8. This provision may also have been included to address the potential problems relating to the use of s.45 of the *Constitution Act, 1982* to amend Alberta's constitution and the initial desire to use the s.43 process. These issues are discussed at page 81 of this book.

337. Section 88 of the *Indian Act, supra,* note 8 incorporates by reference provincial law that affects "Indianess" as federal law and renders it applicable to Indian people in absence of conflict with treaty rights or federal legislation. As a result of this provision, Canadian courts have held that provincial law can limit the exercise of aboriginal rights, but it is not clear whether such legislation has the effect of extinguishing or merely regulating the right (the latter is the stronger argument). Subject to this limited and controversial exception, s.91(24) arguably gives Parliament exclusive jurisdiction over the aboriginal rights of aboriginal peoples within the definition of "Indians." Provincial involvement on Metis issues has historically presumed if Metis had aboriginal rights, they were extinguished. See for example, discussion of the Ewing Commission at page 5. The negotiation of the present legislation presumes that any reference to aboriginal rights invokes the issues of definition and process for constitutional amendment, both which take negotiations out of the provincial realm

and require participation by the federal and other provincial governments, see, *supra*, note 314.

338. [1990] 3 C.N.L.R. 1276 at 134.

339. S. Mellan, "Section 35(3) of the Constitutional Act, 1982: A Window of Constitutional Opportunity for Alberta's Metis Legislation," (6 December 1990) [unpublished] at 13.

340. Schwartz, *First Principles*, *supra*, note 322 at 224.

341. *Supra*, note 339 at 15.

342. *Supra*, note 338 at 150.

343. *Supra*, note 340 at 285.

344. *Constitution of Alberta Amendment Act*, *supra*, note 1, s.5 and 7.

345. For a further discussion *see* R. Elliott, "Rethinking Manner and Form: From Parliamentary Sovereignty to Constitutional Values," *Osgoode Hall Law Journal* 29 (1991): 215.

346. *Constitution Act*, 1982, *supra*, note 10, s.38.

# Appendix 1
# Individual Settlement Maps

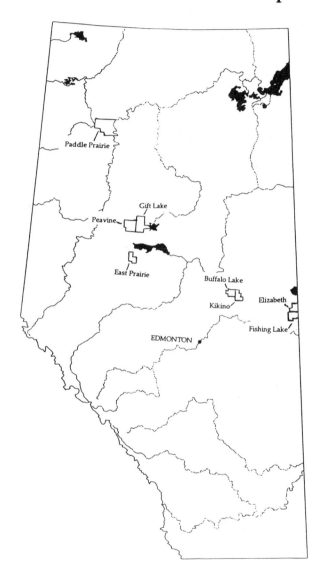

Map of Alberta showing the location of the eight Metis settlements.

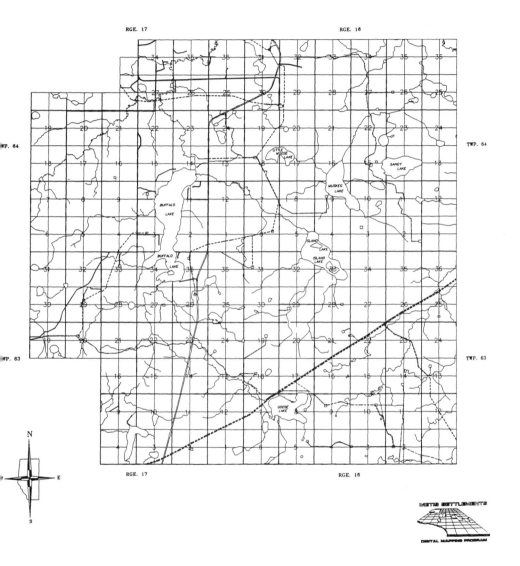

Buffalo Lake Metis Settlement.

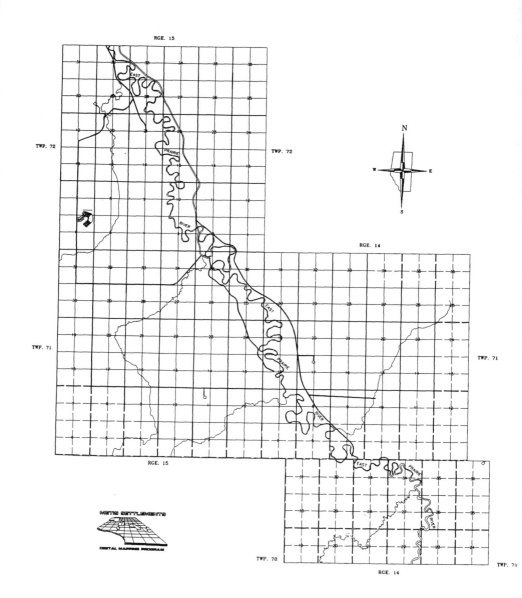

East Prairie Metis Settlement.

104

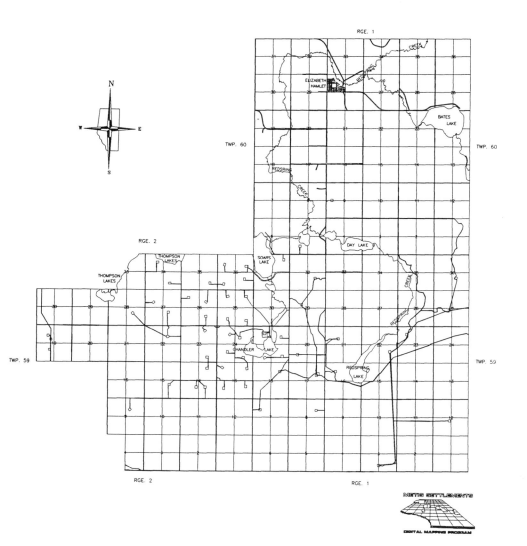

Elizabeth Metis Settlement.

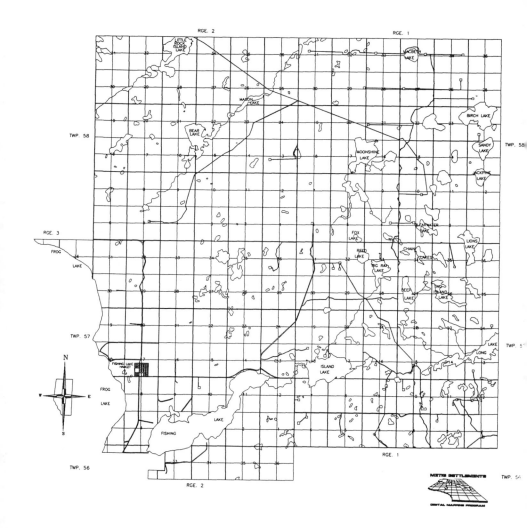

Fishing Lake Metis Settlement.

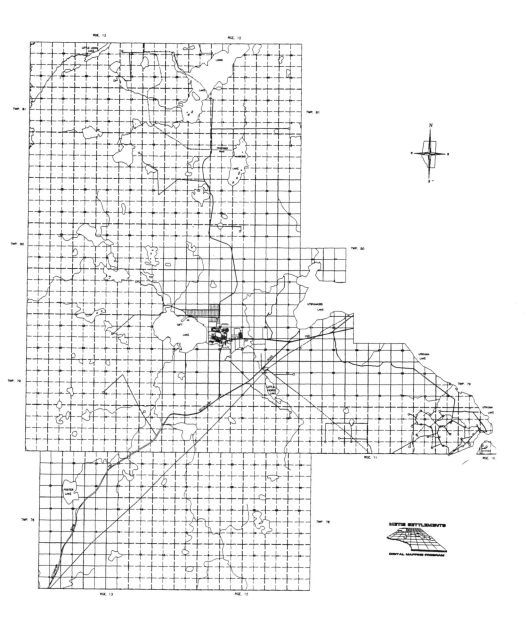

Gift Lake Metis Settlement.

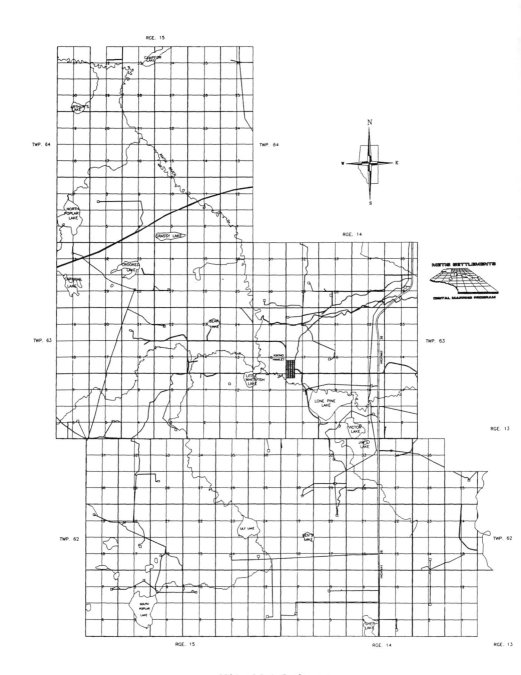

Kikino Metis Settlement.

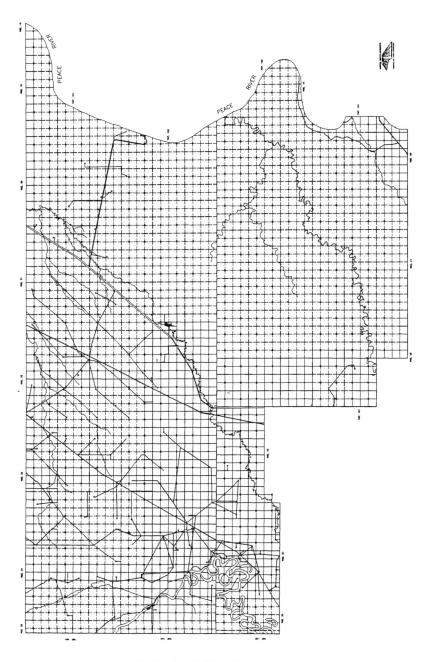

Paddle Prairie Metis Settlement.

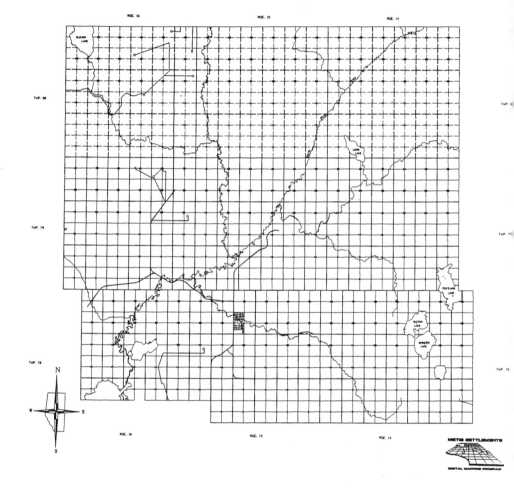

Peavine Metis Settlement.

110

# Appendix 3

## Regulations

Buffalo Lake Metis Settlement Election Regulation, Alta. Reg. 175/91

Land Interests Conversion Regulation, Alta. Reg. 362/91

Metis Settlements Land Registry Regulation, Alta. Reg. 361/91

Metis Settlements Subdivision Regulation, Alta. Reg. 363/91

Time Periods Transitional Regulation, Alta. Reg. 364/91

Transitional Membership Regulation, Alta. Reg. 337/90

## GENERAL COUNCIL POLICIES

### Published

General Council Annual Financial Allocation Policy (No. G.C.P. 91003), *Alberta Gazette,* 1991, I.1754

General Council Census Policy (No. G.C.P. 92011), *Alberta Gazette,* 1992, I.3186

General Council Commercial Activities Policy (No. G.C.P. 90005) *Alberta Gazette,* 1992, I.2621; 3188

General Council Hunting, Fishing, Trapping and Gathering Policy (No. G.C.P. 90001) O.C. 642/90, *Alberta Gazette,* 1991, I.1719

General Council Land Policy (No. G.C.P. 90003), *Alberta Gazette,* 1992, I.2592

General Council Levies Policy (No. G.C.P. 91002), *Alberta Gazette,* 1992, I.2625

General Council Timber Policy (No. G.C.P. 90002), *Alberta Gazette,* 1991, I.1760

General Council Interim Assessment, Levy and Industrial Tax Policy (No. G.C.P. 92001), *Alberta Gazette,* 1993, I.156

### Approved General Council

General Council Annual Financial Allocation Policy (No. G.C.P. 91003)

General Council Financial Interest Policy (No. G.C.P. 92002)

General Council Purposes of Transition Funding

General Council Rules and Procedures Policy

# Appendix 4

Approved and Ordered,
W. HELEN HUNLEY,
Lieutenant Governor.                                    Edmonton, November 15, 1990

Upon the recommendation of the Honourable Ken Rostad, the Lieutenant Governor in Council, pursuant to section 226 of the Metis Settlements Act, approves the attached Metis Settlements General Council Hunting, Fishing, Trapping and Gathering Policy.

Don R. Getty, Chairman.

GCR90-2

## METIS SETTLEMENTS GENERAL COUNCIL
### Unanimous resolution of the General Council
### Hunting, Fishing, Trapping, Gathering Policy

:That the Metis Settlements General Council accept and adopt General Council Policy No. GC90001, entitled Metis Settlements General Council Hunting, Fishing, Trapping and Gathering Policy, a policy to regulate and control the hunting, killing and taking of wildlife and fish, and the gathering of plants in settlement areas.

Approved on November 1st, 1990 at Edmonton, Alberta.

President_____

Secretary_____

Policy GC90001

## METIS SETTLEMENTS GENERAL COUNCIL
## HUNTING, FISHING, TRAPPING AND GATHERING POLICY
## PART 1 - CONTEXT

### 1.1 Background

This policy is made under Section 226(2) of the *Metis Settlements Act*.

### 1.2 Purpose

The purpose of this Policy is to provide for the use, preservation and protection of wildlife, fish and wild plants so that the settlement areas will continue to provide a base for traditional Metis pursuits.

### 1.3 Definitions

In this Policy

- *Act* means the *Metis Settlements Act*;
- *fur-bearing animal* means a fur-bearing animal as defined under the *Wildlife Act*;
- *hunt* means hunt as defined in the *Wildlife Act*;
- *to trap* means to capture in a trap or snare;
- *wild plants* means naturally occuring plants used for food, medicine, spiritual or other traditional pursuits, and does not include trees suitable for logging;
- *wildlife* means wildlife as defined under the *Wildlife Act*;

and all other words defined in the Act have the same meaning in this Policy.

### 1.4 Game preserves

In order to implement the purpose of this Policy a settlement can pass by-laws reserving parts of the settlement area as game preserves and providing for the maintenance and development of fish, wildlife, and wild plants in those preserves.

### 1.5 Special permits

Provided that it is enabled by a settlement by-law, a settlement can issue special permits

(a) to allow the immediate family of a member to hunt, fish or trap in the settlement area;

(b) to allow other non-members to hunt or fish for specified animals or fish at specified times or places

### 1.6 Settlement by-laws

Any settlement bylaw with respect to hunting, fishing, trapping or gathering must be consistent with the provisions of Part 2 of this Policy.

## PART 2 - SETTLEMENT BY-LAW PROVISIONS

### 2.1 Non-members

No one can hunt, fish or trap in the settlement area unless they are a member with a license or are the holder of a special permit.

### 2.2 Licenses

Any member can get a Metis Game License, Metis Food Fishing License, or Metis Trapper's License from the settlement office allowing them to hunt, fish or trap in the settlement area.

### 2.3 Hunting for food

(1) Any member with a Metis Game License can hunt wildlife in the settlement area during any season in order to provide food for their family.

(2) Hunting wildlife for any other purpose is subject to the *Wildlife Act*.

(3) Any hunting in a settlement area is subject to local by-laws, including restrictions on hunting in game preserves.

## 2.4 Trapping

(1) Any member with a Metis Trapper's License can trap fur-bearing animals in the settlement area.

(2) Any trapping within a settlement area is subject to by-laws, including restrictions on trapping in game preserves.

(3) Any selling or disposing of a fur or wildlife hide taken in the settlement area must follow a procedure approved by the settlement council.

## 2.5 Unauthorized traps or snares

Anyone who finds a trap or snare belonging to someone without a Metis Trapper's License can take the trap or snare to the settlement office to be dealt with as the settlement council sees fit.

## 2.6 Gathering of Wild Plants

Subject to local by-laws and the laws of trespass, a member can gather wild plants and their produce within the settlement area during any season.

## 2.7 Application of model by-law

The model by-law set out in Schedule 1 applies to all settlement areas.

## SETTLEMENT HUNTING, FISHING AND TRAPPING BY-LAW
## PART 1 - CONTEXT

### 1.1 Purpose

The purpose of this by-law is to provide for the use, preservation and protection of wildlife, fish and wild plants so that the settlement area will continue to provide a base for traditional Metis pursuits.

### 1.2 Definition

In this by-law

- *Act* means the *Metis Settlements Act*;
- *fur-bearing animal* means a fur-bearing animal as defined under the *Wildlife Act*;
- *hunt* means hunt as defined in the *Wildlife Act*;
- *to trap* means to capture in a trap or snare;
- *wild plants* means naturally occurring plants used for food, medicine, spiritual or other traditional pursuits, and does not include trees suitable for logging;
- *wildlife* means wildlife as defined under the *Wildlife Act*;

and all other words defined in the Act have the same meaning in this by-law.

## PART 2 - CONTENT

### 2.1 Non-members

(1) No one except a member, or the holder of a special permit, can hunt, fish or trap in the settlement area.

(2) The settlement council can approve special permits

(a) to allow someone in the immediate family of a member to hunt, fish or trap in the settlement area;

(b) to allow other non-members to hunt or fish for specified animals or fish at specified times or places.

## 2.2 Licenses

(1) Any member can get a Metis Game License, Metis Food Fishing License or Metis Trapper's License at no charge from the settlement office allowing them to hunt, fish or trap in the settlement area.

(2) All hunting, fishing and trapping licenses expire at the end of March of each year.

## 2.3 Hunting for food

(1) Any member with a Metis Game License can hunt in the settlement area during any season in order to provide food for their family.

(2) Hunting wildlife for any other purpose is subject to the *Wildlife Act*.

(3) Any hunting in a settlement area is subject to local by-laws, including restrictions on hunting in game preserves.

## 2.4 Trapping

(1) Any member with a Metis Trapper's License can trap or kill fur-bearing animals in the settlement area.

(2) Any trapping within a settlement area is subject to by-laws, including restrictions on trapping in game preserves.

(3) Any selling or disposing of a fur or wildlife hide taken in the settlement area must follow a procedure approved by the settlement council.

## 2.5 Unauthorized traps or snares

Anyone who finds a trap or snare belonging to someone without a Metis Trapper's License can take the trap or snare to the settlement office to be dealt with as the settlement council sees fit.

## 2.6 Gathering of Wild Plants

Subject to local by-laws and the laws of trespass, a member can gather wild plants and their produce within the settlement area during any season.

## 2.7 Cancelling licenses

(1) The settlement council can cancel the hunting, fishing and trapping privileges of a member who is convicted of an offence under this by-law or the *Wildlife Act*.

(2) Anyone whose privileges are cancelled under subsection (1) can be denied any right to hunt, fish or trap in the settlement area for up to 5 years.

## 2.8 Offences and penalties

(1) A person who contravenes any provision of this by-law is guilty of an offence.

(2) A person convicted of an offence under this by-law is liable to a fine of not more than $2500.

*Reproduced from *The Alberta Gazette* 87, no. 12 (29 June 1991).

# Appendix 5

## METIS SETTLEMENTS GENERAL COUNCIL LAND POLICY
## PART 1 - CONTEXT

### 1.1 Background

Her Majesty has issued letters patent to the Metis Settlements General Council for the fee simple estate in Metis settlement land. Under the *Metis Settlements Act*, the only rights and interests in this land are those made possible by statute, General Council Policy, or settlement by-law.[1] The *Act* also provides that the General Council can, after consultation with the Minister, make Policies with respect to a number of land related matters, including the creation, transfer and termination of rights in land in the settlement areas.[2]

This Policy is made by the Metis Settlements General Council to provide a framework for the ownership and management of interests in land in the settlement areas.

### 1.2 Purpose

The purpose of this Policy is:

(a) to provide a basic system of interests in Metis settlement land;

(b) to establish principles governing how those interests can be created and passed from one person to another;[3] and

(c) to create a land management system that recognizes and balances the individual rights of the landholder and the collective rights of the settlement as a Metis community.

### 1.3 Definitions

In this Policy:

(a) *Act* means the *Metis Settlements Act*;

(b) *improvements* means changes people have intentionally made to the land in order to increase its usefulness, and includes all structures permanently attached to the land;[4]

(c) *land* includes improvements;

(d) *Metis settlement land* means land held in fee simple by the General Council under letters patent issued by the Crown;[5]

(e) *parcel* means a unit of land for which there is a Metis title register in the Registry;

(f) *Registrar* means the Registrar of the Metis Settlements Land Registry;

(g) *registered* means entered in a register of the Registry in order to complete the process of registration;

(h) *Registry* means the land registry established under the *Metis Settlements Land Registry Regulation*;

(i) *road* means a road allowance, or a road shown on a plan filed with the Registrar;

(j) *settlement held land* means land for which the settlement holds the Metis title;

(k) *transfer* means:

(i) the process, and document, by which a person creates or assigns an interest in land; and

(ii) the process by which the law creates or passes an interest, including the passing of an interest to a personal representative and the passing of an interest by operation of a General Council Policy;[6]

and all other words defined in the *Act* or the *Metis Settlements Land Registry Regulation* have the same meaning in this Policy.

### 1.4 Endnotes [see pages 135-37]

The endnotes in this Policy are a part of the Policy included to help with interpretation.

## PART 2 - INTERESTS IN LAND

### 2.1 Purpose and scope

(1) The purpose of this Part is to establish and describe certain basic interests in Metis settlement land.

(2) This Part applies to all Metis settlement land.

### 2.2 Metis title created

This Policy creates a *Metis title* interest in all Metis settlement land except for roads and the beds and shores of water bodies.[7]

### 2.3 Holder of Metis title

(1) The Metis title in each parcel in a settlement area is held by the settlement unless registered in the name of a member.

(2) If a person who cannot legally hold the Metis title is registered as the holder, the settlement holds the Metis title in trust for the person the law determines should hold it.

### 2.4 Nature of Metis title

(1) Subject to this Policy[8] and settlement by-laws, the holder of the Metis title in a parcel has the exclusive right:

(a) to use and occupy the land;[9]

(b) to make improvements to the land;

(c) to transfer the Metis title;

(d) to grant lesser interests as set out in this Policy;[10] and

(e) to determine who receives the Metis title on the holder's death.

(2) The holder of the Metis title also has any additional rights with respect to the

parcel that are specifically provided for by a General Council Policy or any other enactment.

(3) The Metis title is subject to the following interests whether or not they are registered:

(a) natural rights of light, air, water and support;

(b) traditional community pathways and uses.[11]

(4) In order to clarify traditional pathways and uses a settlement can pass a by-law locating and describing them for settlement held land.

### 2.5 Nature of provisional Metis title

(1) The settlement council can grant a settlement member provisional Metis title in settlement held land to enable the member to use the land and make improvements to the extent needed to obtain Metis title.

(2) A provisional Metis title can only be granted in land for which the settlement holds the Metis title.

(3) The provisional Metis title in a parcel in a settlement area can only be held by the settlement, or someone who is a member of the settlement and has signed a Memorandum of Provisional Metis Title for the parcel.

(4) A Memorandum of Provisional Metis Title must state

(a) the conditions, including improvements to be made to the land, which if met will give the holder the right to acquire the Metis title;

(b) how much time the holder has to satisfy the conditions and what rights of renewal, if any, there are if the conditions are not met in time;

(c) what rights and duties the holder has with respect to the land; and

(d) any other matters that are specified by settlement by-law, regulation or General Council Policy.

(5) A Memorandum of Provisional Metis Title must be in the form attached to this Policy.

(6) Subject to this Policy, settlement by-laws, and the terms of the Memorandum, the holder of the provisional Metis title in a parcel has the exclusive right to use and occupy the land for the purpose of improving the land as required to obtain Metis title.

### 2.6 Nature of an allotment

(1) A settlement can grant an allotment in settlement held land to a member to operate a farm, ranch or business.

(2) An allotment can only be granted in land for which the settlement holds the Metis title.

(3) An allotment in a parcel in a settlement area can only be held by the settlement, or someone who is a member of the settlement and has signed a Memorandum of Allotment for the parcel.

(4) A Memorandum of Allotment must state

(a) the period of time for which the allotment is granted;

(b) the allotment holder's rights of renewal, if any;

(c) the rights and duties of the allotment holder with respect to the land; and

(d) any other matters that are specified by settlement by-law, regulation or General Council Policy.

(5) A Memorandum of Allotment must be in the form attached to this Policy.

(6) Subject to this Policy, settlement by-laws, and the terms of the Memorandum, the holder of an allotment has the exclusive right to use and occupy the land.

## 2.7 Road titles

(1) The settlement holds a non-transferable *road title* interest in each road over which the settlement council has the right of direction, control and management.[12]

(2) A settlement council can grant any interest out of its road title, except Metis title, that General Council Policy allows to be granted for other settlement lands.

(3) A settlement council can create a road title in settlement held land by filing a plan with the Registrar and when it is created the Metis title in that land is terminated.

(4) The settlement council can terminate a road title by notice to the Registrar and the termination of the road title creates a Metis title in the land in the name of the settlement.

## 2.8 Leases by Metis title holder

(1) Subject to the conditions of this Policy, the holder of a Metis title can lease the land to any person.[13]

(2) No lease can be granted that, together with renewal rights, would exceed 10 years, unless the lease is specifically approved by a by-law stating the general nature of the lease and how long it could last if renewal rights were exercised.

(3) A member cannot lease land to a person who is not a member without the settlement council's approval.

## 2.9 Acquiring other rights in settlement held land

(1) The settlement council can create covenants, or grant any person a licence, easement, or utility right of way,[14] in settlement held land.

(2) A grant of a right under this section that could, with renewal rights, last for more than 10 years, has no effect unless approved by a by-law stating the nature of the grant and how long it could last.

(3) This section does not apply to the granting of interests in land, or the right to use land, for the purpose of developing oil, gas or other minerals.

## 2.10 Lesser interests in member held land

(1) A member who holds the Metis title to a parcel, can, with the approval of the settlement council, create a covenant or grant a license, easement, or utility right of way, on the parcel.

(2) A grant of an interest under this section that could, with renewal rights, last for more than 10 years, has no effect unless the grant is approved by a by-law stating the nature of the grant and how long it could last.

## 2.11 Granting rights of removal

(1) Subject to settlement by-laws and General Council Policies on resource development, a settlement council can:

(a) grant rights of removal for non-renewable contents of the soil[15] from any parcel of land in the settlement area; and

(b) grant a right of access to any land in the settlement area to effect the removal.

(2) The Metis title holder's exclusive right to use and occupy land[16] is subject to the right of access granted under subsection (1)(b).

(3) Any benefit[17] resulting from a grant under subsection (1) belongs to the settlement.

(4) If the interests of someone other than the settlement are damaged by the removal, they are entitled to fair compensation for their loss.

(5) If the settlement and the person whose interests are damaged cannot agree on what is fair compensation, either one can refer the matter to the Appeal Tribunal.

(6) In deciding how much compensation the person is entitled to the Appeal Tribunal can consider the damage to the person's interests and any other matters it considers relevant.

## 2.12 Registerable interests

The following interests may be registered, as well as recorded, in the Registry:

(a) a Metis title, provisional Metis title, or allotment;

(b) a road title, easement, covenant, or utility right of way;

(c) a lease;

(d) a charge against the interest of a non-member;

(e) an estate under the *Dower Act*;[18]

(f) a right of removal granted under section 2.11.

## 2.13 Recording of interim allocations

(1) In this section *interim allocation* means an interest in land that was either:

(a) granted to a member under the former Act but not shown in the Minister's records; or

(b) granted to a member on or after November 1, 1990, but before the coming into force of the *Metis Settlements Land Registry Regulation*.

(2) An interim allocation may be recorded in the Registry.

(3) An interim allocation is deemed to be an allocation under the *Land Interests Conversion Regulation* and may only be extinguished, or converted to a Metis title, allotment, or provisional Metis title, in accordance with that regulation.

## PART 3 - LIMITATIONS AND IMPLIED INTERESTS

### 3.1 Purpose and scope
(1) The purpose of this Part is to describe limitations and conditions on the basic interests in Metis settlement land.

(2) This Part applies to all Metis settlement land.

### 3.2 Limits on interests
(1) The holder of a Metis title, provisional Metis title, or allotment in a parcel has the right to make direct use of the timber and non-renewable resources found in the parcel to make improvements to the parcel.[19]

(2) The Metis title does not include any rights[20] to timber or non-renewable resources[21] other than those set out in subsection (1).

### 3.3 Limits on length of grants
(1) Unless provided for in this Policy, or in a settlement by-law made under a General Council Policy that specifically allows a longer term,[22] neither the settlement nor a member can grant an interest in land that, including renewal rights, could exceed 10 years, and any such grant is void.

(2) A settlement can provide by by-law that if a member is operating a farm, ranch, or business on the land at the end of the term of an allotment, and has made permanent improvements to the land for that purpose, he or she can apply to renew the allotment or any extension of it for 5 more years and on the application have some form of priority over other applicants.

### 3.4 Limits on amount of land held by Metis title
(1) Subject to subsection (2), no member can hold the Metis title to parcels with a total area of more than 175 acres.

(2) A member can hold the Metis title to more than 175 acres of land if the additional land consists of one parcel of no more than 167 acres and the additional parcel is used and required by the member to operate a farm, ranch or business.

(3) The number of hamlet lots that a member can hold by Metis title is at most one.

(4) This section does not apply to limit the amount of land a person can hold for the purpose of acting as a Land Trustee under the provisions of Part 7.

### 3.5 Implied terms of lease
Every non-residential lease[23] of land in a settlement area, unless it clearly says otherwise in writing, includes the following implied terms in the lease agreement:

- The person granting the lease promises:
  I will let you use the land[24] without interference as long as you pay the rent and live up to the terms of the lease agreement;

- The person receiving the lease promises:
  (1) I will pay the rent when, and in the way, the agreement requires;

  (2) I will pay any charges, levies or taxes related to the ownership or use of the land during the lease;

(3) I will take care of the land[25] and return it in good condition at the end of the lease;

(4) If the land includes farm land, I will work it according to good farming practice;

(5) If given reasonable notice, I will let you or your representative enter the land to inspect its condition;

(6) If given written notice that I am not living up to the agreement, I will correct the situation within a reasonable time; and if I have not corrected it within 2 months I will let you take the land back without interference.

### 3.6 No multiple holders of interests

(1) The Metis title, allotment or provisional Metis title in a parcel cannot be held by more than one person at a time.[26]

(2) Any transfer contrary to subsection (1) is void.

### 3.7 Non-renewable resources

(1) Subject to subsection (2), a Metis title holder may grant any lease, licence, easement, or right of way required to

(a) explore for or develop non-renewable resources, or

(b) implement authorized projects or development agreements[27] as defined in the *Act*.

(2) The grant can only be made if it is of a class permitted by settlement by-law and the settlement council approves the specific grant.

(3) The limits of section 3.3(1) do not apply to this section, and the rights granted under subsection (1) may be for as long a term as required to make the project viable.

## PART 4 - GRANTING INTERESTS IN SETTLEMENT HELD LAND

### 4.1 Purpose and scope

(1) The purpose of this Part is to provide guidelines for fair and orderly procedures when granting new interests in settlement land held.

(2) This part does not apply to grants of

(a) licences, easements, rights of removal,[28] or rights of way;

(b) leases that, together with any right of renewal, are for a term of 5 years or less;

(c) interests required for the exploration or development of oil, gas, or other non-renewable resources;

(d) Metis title to the holder of a provisional Metis title or an allotment.

### 4.2 Making settlement held land available

The settlement council can decide, in accordance with this Policy and settlement by-laws:

(a) what parcels of settlement held land should be made available for use or development;

(b) the purposes for which they should be made available; and

(c) the type of interest that should be granted or transferred to enable the desired use or development.

### 4.3 Notice of available land

(1) If the settlement council decides that an interest in settlement held land should be made available, it must provide at least 14 days public notice of the availability of the interest and the application requirements.

(2) The notice must state, for each parcel in which an interest is to be made available:

(a) the legal description of the parcel;

(b) the interest being offered, including any conditions or limitations on the interest;

(c) the purpose for which the interest is being made available;

(d) the deadline for submitting an application;

(e) the persons who are eligible to apply for the interest; and

(f) any special conditions that must be met as part of the application.

### 4.4 Applications

(1) Any person who is eligible to apply for a posted interest in settlement held land can file an application in the required form at the settlement office.

(2) The application must

(a) be signed by the applicant seeking the interest;

(b) clearly identify the posted interest being sought;

(c) indicate that the applicant accepts the limitations or conditions set out in the posting;

(d) indicate that the applicant understands that although the settlement council may approve an application it is subject to appeal and is uncertain until the appeal process has concluded;

(e) include any required application fees or deposits; and

(f) satisfy any other application requirements established by settlement by-law.

### 4.5 Considerations

When considering an application for an interest in settlement held land, the settlement council can take into account:

(a) the applicant's ability and commitment to use the interest for the intended purpose;

(b) the extent to which the applicant will require financial assistance from the settlement to develop the land for the intended use;

(c) the extent of the applicant's existing debt to the settlement and the likelihood that it will be paid;

(d) the amount the applicant is prepared to pay;

(e) whether granting the interest to the applicant is consistent with the settlement's by-laws;

(f) whether the interest can be registered in the name of the applicant; and

(g) any other criteria established by settlement by-law.

### 4.6 Applying for an allotment

In addition to the factors set out in section 4.5, in deciding whether to approve an application for an allotment the settlement council can consider:

(a) the extent to which the settlement area is, and has been, the applicant's real home and residence;

(b) whether the applicant has been and is currently using the land for the intended purpose;

(c) the extent to which the applicant needs the land to operate a viable farm, ranch or business; and

(d) any other criteria established by settlement by-law.

### 4.7 Decisions

(1) The settlement council must provide notice[29] of its decisions on the granting of interests within 45 days of the posted deadline for applications.

(2) The settlement council may accept an application or reject all applications for the posted interest.

## PART 5 - CHANGES IN INTEREST HOLDER

### 5.1 Purpose and scope

(1) The purpose of this Part is to set out procedures for the acquisition of interests in land in a way that will respect the rights of the individual and the rights of the community.

(2) This part applies only to the acquisition[30] of Metis title, provisional Metis title, and allotments.

### 5.2 Acquiring Metis title from the settlement

(1) Any member who holds a parcel by provisional Metis title or by an allotment can apply at the settlement office for the Metis title to the parcel.

(2) The settlement council must approve the transfer of Metis title to the applicant if:

(a) the applicant is a member who is living in the settlement area;

(b) the applicant has no overdue debts owed to the settlement;

(c) the applicant would, if the Metis title were transferred, not exceed the land holding limits;

(d) the applicant is living on the land or operating a business, farm or ranch on it; and

(e) the land has been improved

(i) by constructing a house or permanent business buildings on it; or

(ii) by fencing, clearing, cultivating, or otherwise working a significant part of the land to enhance its productive capacity.

(3) A settlement may, by by-law, provide more details for the conditions set out in 5.2(2)(d) or 5.2(2)(e).

(4) Within 45 days of receiving the application, the settlement council must either

(a) notify[31] the applicant that the conditions for transferring Metis title have not been met; or

(b) provide the applicant with a transfer of Metis title.

### 5.3 Acquisition of interests

(1) In order to acquire an interest, a notice in the form prescribed by the Registrar's rules must be filed with the settlement administrator.

(2) The settlement administrator must provide the applicant and the Registrar with a copy of the notice showing the date and time it was received.

(3) Within 14 days[32] of receiving the notice the settlement administrator must notify the applicant and the Registrar in writing if the acquisition requires review by the settlement council.

(4) If not notified within 14 days, the Registrar may assume that the council has no objection.

(5) This section does not apply if the interest is being acquired from the settlement.

### 5.4 Objections to acquisitions

(1) A settlement council can object to an acquisition if it

(a) decides that the acquisition is contrary to settlement land use or land management by-laws; and

(b) notifies the applicant and the Registrar in writing that the settlement objects to the acquisition.

(2) The objection is not valid unless

(a) the settlement administrator has given the notice required under section 5.3(3), and

(b) the applicant and Registrar are notified within 45 days of the date the acquisition is filed with the settlement administrator.

### 5.5 Settlement council authority

A settlement council can establish additional rules governing the acquisition of interests in land in the settlement area, provided the rules are set out in a land management by-law that is consistent with this Policy.

# PART 6 - LOSING AN INTEREST IN LAND

## 6.1 Purpose and scope

(1) The purpose of this Part is to provide guidelines for the process of terminating a person's interests in land so that there is a fair balance of the rights of the individual and the rights of the community.

(2) In this Part, unless the context requires a different interpretation,

(a) *interest* means a Metis title, provisional Metis title, or allotment;

(b) *settlement council* means the settlement council of the settlement area in which the affected land is located.

## 6.2 Cancelling interests in land

(1) The settlement council can require the sale of an interest in a parcel, or apply for the subdivision of a parcel and require the sale of interests in subdivided parcels, if the holder of the interest, in spite of warnings, fails to pay charges, levies or taxes that are owed to the settlement in relation to the ownership of the interest.

(2) The settlement council cannot decide to require a subdivision or sale of an interest under this section without first giving the holder at least 60 days notice of when and where it will meet to consider the matter, and a chance to be heard.

(3) If the settlement council decides that a subdivision or sale is necessary, the settlement council must notify the holder and the Registrar.

(4) The settlement's right to have the land subdivided or sold is an interest that may be recorded in the Registry.

(5) Once the settlement's notice of required subdivision or sale has been recorded, and until it has been cancelled, the interest holder cannot grant any rights in the parcel unless the grant is approved in writing by the settlement council.

(6) On receiving a notice under subsection (3), the interest holder has 60 days to appeal to the Appeal Tribunal and no appeal of the decision can be made after that.

(7) The termination of a person's interest in land under subsection (1) does not affect the status of any registered or recorded interests acquired from that person.

## 6.3 Sale of interest

(1) An interest holder receiving a notice under 6.2(3) to sell an interest has 1 year to arrange the sale.

(2) The interest can be sold to the settlement if the holder and the settlement council can agree to terms.

(3) If, within that year, the interest holder pays all the charges, levies, taxes and related costs that are the basis for the settlement's notice the settlement's related right to require sale or subdivision ends and the settlement must request the cancellation of the corresponding recording.

### 6.4 Auction

(1) If a person has not sold the interest within 1 year of receiving notice under section 6.2(3), the settlement council can inform the Registrar and the Registrar must cancel the existing registration of the interest and register the interest in the name of the settlement.

(2) The settlement council must auction the interest[33] as soon as reasonably possible after it has been registered in the name of the settlement.

(3) The settlement council can retain the interest and refuse any bid unless:

(a) the bid is from a member eligible to acquire the interest, and

(b) the bid would allow the settlement to recover debts owed to it by the former interest holder in relation to that interest.

(4) Any proceeds left from the auction of the interest, after the costs of the auction and the debts registered against the interest have been paid, must be paid to the person who has lost the interest.

## PART 7 - DESCENT OF PROPERTY

### 7.1 Purpose and scope

(1) The purpose of this Part is to provide basic rules governing the transfer of a member's interests in land when he or she dies.[34]

(2) As far as possible this Part should be applied in a way that:

(a) recognizes the communal interests of the settlement, and

(b) enables settlement members to determine who will receive the benefit of their interests in land when they die.

(3) This Part applies only to Metis settlement land and interests held by members.

### 7.2 Definitions

In this Part:

- *deceased's spouse* means an individual who at the time of the deceased's death

  (a) was lawfully married to the deceased, or

  (b) lived with the deceased as husband or wife and was treated as such by the community;

- *estate instructions* means written instructions, filed with the Registrar, saying what should be done with a member's interests in land when he or she dies;

- *extended family* means all living persons who

  (a) are in the deceased's immediate family,

  (b) are descended from someone in the deceased's immediate family, or

  (c) are the deceased's brother, sister, father, mother or grandchild;

- *heirs list* means a list of persons named in estate instructions in order of priority for consideration to receive interests in land when the holder dies;

- *homestead* means the parcel of land where the house in which the Metis title holder lives is located;
- *immediate family* means the spouse and children of the deceased;
- *land trustee* means the person holding a deceased member's interests in land while the estate instructions are carried out.

### 7.3 Staying on the homestead

(1) Nothing in this Part affects any rights provided by the *Dower Act* or settlement by-law that would enable a deceased's spouse to continue living on the homestead when the Metis title holder dies.

(2) For the purposes of the *Dower Act*, a deceased's spouse, whether a member or not, may acquire "an estate for the life of the spouse" in the homestead.

(3) A non-member who holds an "estate for the life of the spouse" cannot grant any interest in the homestead without the approval of the settlement council.

### 7.4 *Family Relief Act*

Nothing in this part affects the rights of a deceased's family under the *Family Relief Act*.

### 7.5 Wills not effective

(1) No provision of a will relating to a member's interest in Metis settlement land has any effect.

(2) The *Wills Act*, the *Devolution of Real Property Act*, and the *Administration of Estates Act* do not apply to the interests of a member in Metis settlement land.

### 7.6 Estate instructions

(1) The owner of an interest in land may at any time file with the Registrar

    (a) estate instructions, or

    (b) changes in estate instructions

for that interest.

(2) The Registrar must accept the instructions or changes for filing if they are in the form set out in Schedule 1, or any other form recommended by the Registrar and approved by the General Council.

(3) Estate instructions may

    (a) name a land trustee;

    (b) provide an heirs list stating, in order of preference, who is to get the deceased's interest in the land and what to do with the interest if no one on the list takes it; or

    (c) give directions to sell the interest and put the money from the sale in the deceased's estate.

(4) The Registrar may accept estate instructions that are not made on the required form, if the instructions contain enough of the information set out in subsection (3) to provide direction.

## 7.7 Confidentiality

All estate instructions received by the Registrar are confidential and may only be released at the written request of the interest holder, or on that person's death, at the written request of a member of the deceased's immediate family, the settlement council, the land trustee or the administrator of the deceased's estate.

## 7.8 Effect of instructions

Any estate instruction providing for the transfer of part, but not all, of the deceased's interest in the land has no effect.

## 7.9 Appointing a land trustee

(1) Instructions to the Registrar to register an interest in land may name a member, or the settlement, as land trustee to hold the interest when the applicant dies and arrange for its transfer to the proper person.

(2) When the registered holder of an interest dies, and there is a land trustee capable of holding the interest shown in the Registry, the interest passes to the land trustee.

(3) If an interest holder dies without appointing a land trustee, or if when the holder dies the person appointed is unable or unwilling to serve, the settlement is the land trustee unless the settlement council appoints someone else.

## 7.10 Trustee's duties

(1) The land trustee holds the deceased's interest only for the purpose of dealing with the land according to the estate instructions, settlement by-laws, and this Policy.

(2) The land trustee must administer the interest and arrange for its transfer in a way that will, as far as possible, give effect to the wishes of the deceased as set out in the estate instructions.

(3) The settlement council can replace land trustees who fail to carry out their duties.

## 7.11 Registration of trustee

On application, the register must be changed to show the land trustee as holder of the land interests of the deceased for the purpose of administering the estate.

## 7.12 Referral to council

(1) The land trustee must apply to the settlement council for direction

(a) if there are no estate instructions;

(b) if for any reason the estate instructions are uncertain or impossible to carry out; or

(c) if the interest held by the trustee has not been transferred to a person on the heirs list by the 21st anniversary of the deceased's death.

(2) On receiving an application for direction the settlement council can either decide who should receive the deceased's interest or refer the matter to the Appeal Tribunal.

## 7.13 Guiding principles

(1) When an application has been made under section 7.12, any determination of the question, whether by the settlement council or the Appeal Tribunal, must be guided by the following principles in the stated order of priority:

(a) as far as possible, and to the extent that they can be clearly determined, the last wishes of the deceased should be met;[35]

(b) the interest must be transferred to the deceased's spouse if it can be registered in his or her name, and if there is more land than can be registered in the spouse's name the spouse can specify the order in which the interests should be considered for registration;[36]

(c) if there is one or more living adults on the heirs list and they agree on what should be done with the interest, the agreement should be followed;

(d) if it is not possible to get an agreement from the persons on the heirs list but, in the opinion of the body making the decision, there is substantial agreement among adult members of the deceased's family as to what should be done with the interest, that agreement should be followed;

(e) if there are no adult members of the deceased's family, but the deceased leaves living children, the land interest should be given to the child who, in the opinion of the settlement council, is best able to use it for the purpose intended;

(f) if it is not possible within a reasonable time to decide who should receive the interest in accordance with the above principles, the land should be sold and the money made part of the deceased's estate.

(2) In this section "deceased's family" means the adult members of the deceased's immediate family, if there are any, and otherwise the adult members of the deceased's extended family.

## PART 8 - APPEALS AND REFERENCES

## 8.1 Right to appeal

(1) Wherever this Policy requires the General Council or a settlement council to make a decision related to the granting, transfer, or termination of interests in land in the settlement area, any person affected by the decision, or lack of a decision, can appeal in writing to the Appeal Tribunal.

(2) The appeal must be filed with the Appeal Tribunal, and a Notice of Appeal filed with the Registrar, within 30 days of the settlement council's decision, or, if the settlement council did not make a decision, within 30 days of the date by which it was required to have made the decision.

(3) There is no right of appeal if the proper documents are not filed with the Appeal Tribunal and the Registrar within the specified time limit.[37]

## 8.2 References

Any questions or dispute as to the ownership or extent of an interest in land in a settlement area may be referred to the Appeal Tribunal for an advance ruling or for a decision.[38]

# PART 9 - GENERAL

## 9.1 Informing the Registrar

When a settlement council makes a by-law, or the General Council makes a Policy, affecting registerable interests in land they must inform the Registrar as soon as possible.

## 9.2 Previous Policy rescinded

This Policy rescinds and replaces all previous General Council Land Policies.

# SCHEDULE 1
## ESTATE INSTRUCTIONS

Estate instructions of_____ for the land described
in the land register as_____

I want_____to be my Land Trustee for this land and if that's impossible,
then I want, in order_____or_____or_____.

## CROSS OUT ONE OF OPTION A OR OPTION B

**Option A – Transfer My Interest**
Instructions to my Land Trustee:
**Who should get the land**
My preference as to who should get my interests in this land is:
1.
2.
3.
4.
5.
6.

[If you don't name anyone here, the council will have to decide according to the Policy who should get the land. You can name as many people as you want but if the land has not been transferred within 21 years the council will have to decide who gets it.]

**How to decide who gets it**
Offer the interest to the first person on the list when they are old enough to take it. Give them some time to become eligible to hold the interest and get it registered in their name. If for any reason they don't get it registered within a reasonable time, take their name off the list and start the process over with the next person on the list. Keep doing this until someone gets the interest.

**What to do if no one on the list can get it**
If no one in the list can take the interest then do one of the following: [Circle only one]
- sell this interest and treat the money as part of my estate;
- ask the settlement council to decide who should get it.

**What to do with money paid for using the land**
Make sure that any money paid for using the land before the land is transferred is accounted for, keep a fair amount for your expenses in taking care of the land and carrying out these instructions, and pay the rest to

[If you don't say who the money should go to it will go to the person getting the land when it is transferred.]

---

**Option B – Sell My Interest**
Instructions to my Land Trustee:
As soon as you can, sell my interest for as much as you can get, keep enough to pay for your expenses, and treat the rest of the money as part of my estate.

Date: _____          Signed: _____

Witness: _____

## Endnotes

1.  This provision is found in section 99 of the *Metis Settlements Act*.

2.  Section 222 of the *Metis Settlements Act*.

3.  In this Policy, "person" means a legal entity such as an individual, the settlement or any other incorporated body.

4.  A "structure" is anything built, for example houses, buildings, water systems, and fences. A structure is "permanently attached to the land" if all or part of it is buried in order to attach it to the land and keep it there for the foreseeable future. Things permanently attached to the structure are considered as part of the structure for this purpose.

5.  This is the same definition as given for "patented land" by the *Metis Settlements Land Protection Act*.

6.  So, for example, a transfer would include the passing of an interest on death or a gift of an interest.

7.  Here "roads" includes existing and future roads, and "water bodies" means bodies of water or waterways.

8.  See especially the Council's right to grant access under section 2.11, and the limitations in Part 3.

9.  By the definitions earlier in this Policy, "land" includes improvements such as houses and other buildings.

10. Off the settlements, "lesser interests" include things like a life estate, lease, easement, covenant, licence or right of use. This Policy permits the creation of some of these kinds of interests subject to certain conditions protecting the rights of the community.

11. For example, members may walk down a footpath to the lake as they have been doing regularly for the past 20 years. This would make the footpath a traditional community pathway. Also, members may be using a certain part of the parcel as a berry picking patch, as they have regularly been doing for many years. That would create a traditional community use.

12. The settlement council may have direction, control and management of roads under section 109 of the Act.

13. It is assumed that the holder of Metis title and the person leasing the land will have reached an agreement on the terms of the lease. In the case of a non-residential lease, the terms listed in section 3.5 will be considered as part of the agreement unless the agreement says they don't apply. Also remember that "person" includes an individual or a corporation.

14. In this Policy *"covenant"* means what, in common law, is called a "restrictive covenant". This is essentially a restriction on the use of the land that stays with the land even if the Metis title holder changes. An example might be "At least 10 acres must always be left in its original bush condition." The term "easement" has the usual common law definition. It means essentially allowing a neighbour to use part of your land for a purpose related to the use of their land. An example might be allowing your neighbour to move cattle over a specific part of your land to get to water. The phrase *"utility right of way"* has the same meaning as the term *"utility interest"* in the *Registry Regulation*. It means essentially an interest that makes it possible to install lines, pipes, ditches, and so on for services like electricity, gas, sewage, and irrigation.

15. For example sand, gravel, clay and marl.

16. See subsection 2.4(1)(a).

17. Here "benefit" would include any money paid or other consideration given for the grant.

18. For a description of this estate see section 7.3(3).

19. For example, the person could use trees for fence posts for fencing the land, logs for building a barn, or gravel for gravelling a driveway on the land. They could not sell the trees, timber or gravel to someone to use off the parcel, however.

20. This does not prevent the settlement, or a member, from acquiring rights by some other means established by settlement by-law and General Council Policy. For example, in section 2.11 this Policy says the settlement council can grant rights of removal. The rights to remove timber are set out in the Timber Policy.

21. The term "non-renewable resources" means sand, gravel, peat, clay, marl, oil, gas, minerals, and any other original part of the land that nature does not readily replace.

22. Such as bylaws made under Section 2.8(2), 2.9(2), 2.10(2) and 3.7(1). It is possible that some other General Council Policy, such as the Resource Policy, could provide for a settlement by-law allowing some form of longer interests.

23. If a person leases a self-contained dwelling unit (for example a house) just to live there, the lease is a residential lease. Every other kind of lease is a non-residential lease. So, for example, if someone leases a quarter section of land to someone else to farm, that would be a non-residential lease.

24. In this section "land" includes the buildings and other improvements being leased.

25. As noted above, in these implied terms, "land" includes buildings and other improvements.

26. In particular, this means that an interest cannot be held by "tenants in common" or "joint tenants."

27. The terms "authorized projects" and "development agreements" are defined in section 111 of the *Act*. They relate to the use of land for mineral development and utilities.

28. This refers to a right of removal granted under section 2.11.

29. Here "notice" means posting the decision and mailing notice of the decision to all applicants.

30. This includes acquiring an interest from the settlement or from another member even if the interest is acquired as the result of the member's death.

31. A requirement in this Part to provide written notice to a person will be satisfied if every reasonable effort is made to ensure the person receives the notice in writing or by fax.

32. In this context "14 days" means 14 actual days total, counting the filing day, holidays and weekends. So, for example, if the transfer notice was filed on April 2, the administrator would have to provide a notice of review by midnight April 15th.

33. Because of the limitations on who can hold a Metis title, provisional Metis title, or allotment, only members eligible to hold the interest would be able to bid at the auction.

34. This Policy does not deal with what happens to a member's personal things when he or she dies. If the member leaves a will the things should be dealt with according to the will and the *Wills Act*. If the member dies without a will the things should be dealt with according to the *Intestate Successions Act*.

35. As indicated in the opening words of this section, each subsection only comes into play

if the matter is not resolved by the subsections ahead of it. So, for example, if it is clear that the deceased wanted the land to go to a particular underage child, the body making the decision would have to try to make arrangements so that could happen. The next subsection would not come into play if the deceased's wishes are clear.

36. As indicated in the opening words of this section, each subsection is subject to the subsections ahead of it. So, for example, in this subsection the spouse must be guided by the last wishes of the deceased if those wishes can be clearly determined. Similarly, in the next subsection, if the deceased left clear written instructions that the eldest son was to get the interest, but died before the son was an adult, the family would have to respect those wishes when agreeing on what should be done with the land.

37. Under section 202 of the *Act*, the Appeal Tribunal may extend the time in special circumstances and this could allow it to make sure people with real problems are heard.

38. Section 199 of the *Act* sets out the conditions under which a dispute or reference can be made to the Appeal Tribunal.

# Appendix 6
# Memorandum of Provisional Metis Title

MPMT#: \_\_\_\_\_

The settlement, as holder of the Metis title, grants you, _____, provisional Metis title to the land legally described as _____.

## ON THE FOLLOWING TERMS:

### 1. Possession
(1)  You have the exclusive right to use and occupy the land for 5 years, starting _____and ending_____as long as you are making the improvements needed to get Metis title and are using the land for the purpose of_____.

(2) If you have not received Metis title to the land at the end of the first 5 year term, but in the settlement's opinion you are productively using the land and have made satisfactory progress on improvements, you can renew this grant for one more 5 year term.

### 2. Limits on interest
This grant does not give you any rights to non-renewable resources, timber, roadways or the beds and shores of bodies of water or waterways.

### 3. Conditions
(1) The basic rules for keeping this grant are:

(a) you must remain a resident member of the settlement;

(b) you can only use the land to build a house or operate a farm, ranch or an approved business;

(c) you cannot do anything to the land that does long term damage to it or other land in the settlement area;

(d) if there is a settlement by-law putting levies, user fees or taxes on the land, improvements or interest, you must make the payments required by the by-law;

(e) you cannot give anyone else an interest in the land [for example by leasing it or signing over part of your interest] without the settlement's written consent;

(f) you must obey settlement by-laws when making improvements on the land or operating a business.

(2) If you break one of these basic rules the settlement can end this allotment 60 days after they have given you written notice saying why the allotment is being ended, and when it will end.

(3) Your provisional Metis title ends on the date specified in the notice unless before then you file a Notice of Appeal with the Appeal Tribunal.

## 4. Community need
If the settlement has passed a by-law saying that part or all of this land is needed for some other purpose, this grant can be ended as far as the needed part goes.

## 5. Returning the land
(1) Within 60 days of the end of this grant, unless you are waiting on a decision on an application for Metis title to this land, you must return the land to the settlement in no worse condition than you received it.

(2) Any improvements on the land that are not removed after 60 days become the property of the settlement.

(3) It is completely up to the settlement council to decide whether you should be paid compensation for the improvements you leave, and if it decides you should receive compensation it will decide how much by taking into account how much you paid for the improvements and how much you owe the settlement (including cleanup costs if there are any).

## 6. Obtaining title
(1) While this grant is in effect you can claim the Metis title to the land if

(a) you have made the improvements required by by-law;

(b) you meet the land holding conditions set by by-law;

(c) you have paid all the user fees, levies and other charges on the land or required for the issuing of Metis title; and

(d) you can be registered as the holder of the Metis title.

(2) In subsection (1) by-law means the settlement land use by-law in effect when this grant was given, or if the grant is renewed, in effect when the renewal was given.

(3) The Metis title you get will be subject to the interests registered on it at the Metis Settlements Land Registry.

## 7. Legal matters
(1) If we have a dispute about the terms of this grant we agree to ask the Metis Settlements Appeal Tribunal to appoint an arbitrator to resolve the matter and we agree to be bound by the arbitrator's decision.

(2) If there are any law suits because of what you do on this land, you, and not the settlement, will be responsible.

(3) If you transfer or leave this grant to someone else, their rights and duties are the same as yours.

## 8. Special conditions
This grant is subject to the following special conditions:

_____

_____

_____

_____

Signed _____, 19____ by

Applicant_____

Settlement_____

# Appendix 7
# Memorandum of Allotment

MA#: _____

The settlement, as holder of the Metis title, grants you, _____, an allotment in the land legally described as _____.

## ON THE FOLLOWING TERMS:

### 1. Possession

(1) You have the exclusive right to use and occupy the land for 10 years, starting _____ and ending_____, as long as you are farming, ranching, or operating a business on it.

(2) If you are still operating your farm, ranch or business on the land at the end of the term, and have made permanent improvements to the land for that purpose, you can apply to renew this allotment or any extension of it for 5 more years and you will have priority over other applicants.

### 2. Limits on interest

This grant of an allotment does not give you any rights to non-renewable resources, timber, roadways or the beds and shores of bodies of water or waterways.

### 3. Conditions

(1) The basic rules for keeping this allotment are:

    (a) you must remain a member of the settlement;

    (b) you can only use the land as a place where you farm, ranch or operate an approved business;

    (c) you cannot build a permanent house on this land;

    (d) you cannot do anything to the land that does long term damage to it or other land in the settlement area;

    (e) if there is a settlement by-law putting levies, user fees or taxes on the land, improvements or interest, you must make the payments required by the by-law;

    (f) you cannot give anyone else an interest in the land [for example by leasing it or signing over part of our interest] without the settlement's written consent;

    (g) you must obey settlement by-laws when making improvements on the land or operating a business.

(2) If you break one of these basic rules the settlement can end this allotment 60 days after they have given you written notice saying why the allotment is being ended, and when it will end.

(3) Your allotment ends on the date specified in the notice unless before then you file a Notice of Appeal with the Appeal Tribunal.

## 4. Community need

If the settlement has passed a by-law saying that part or all of this land is needed for some other purpose, this allotment can be ended as far as the needed part goes.

## 5. Returning the land

(1) Within 60 days of the end of this allotment you must return the land to the settlement in no worse condition than you received it.

(2) Any improvements on the land that are not removed after 60 days become the property of the settlement.

(3) It is completely up to the settlement council to decide whether you should be paid compensation for the improvements you leave, and if it decides you should receive compensation it will decide how much by taking into account how much you paid for the improvements and how much you owe the settlement (including cleanup costs if there are any).

## 6. Legal matters

(1) If we have a dispute about the terms of this allotment we agree to ask the Metis Settlements Appeal Tribunal to appoint an arbitrator to resolve the matter and we agree to be bound by the arbitrator's decision.

(2) If there are any law suits because of what you do on this land, you, and not the settlement, will be responsible.

(3) If you transfer or leave this allotment to someone else, their rights and duties are the same as yours.

## 7. Special conditions

This allotment is subject to the following special conditions:

_____

_____

_____

_____

Signed _____, 19___ by

Applicant_____

Settlement_____

# Index

143